Praise for *Moms to Moms*

"*Moms to Moms* warmly welcomes readers into the heart of parenting, with practical advice and uplifting anecdotes covering a wide variety of tasks and concerns. Barbara Joy's wisdom, experience, and love for recovery and parenting shines brightly through each page. I heartily recommend it."

—MARY COOK, MA, RAS, AUTHOR OF *GRACE LOST AND FOUND: FROM ADDICTIONS AND COMPULSIONS TO SATISFACTION AND SERENITY*

"Being a mom is living a role. What every woman wants and needs is an authentic life of her own. So read and learn how to find your life and give birth to your new self."

—BERNIE SIEGEL, MD, AUTHOR OF *LOVE, MAGIC & MUDPIES* AND *PRESCRIPTIONS FOR LIVING*

"These pages offer a community of compassion assuring a mom, 'You are not alone.' Joy masterfully weaves engaging stories from moms all over the country with the threads of her own wise guidance. If you are a mom in recovery, or close to one, this is the book for you."

—MARY ANNE RADMACHER, AUTHOR OF *LEAN FORWARD INTO YOUR LIFE*

With encouragement and wisdom on every page, Barbara Joy and others share a message of hope and empowerment for moms in recovery. Through their touching and courageous stories they exemplify that your history isn't your destiny and that it is never too late to be the person you want to be. This book is a blessing for every soul in recovery."

—STEVE MARABOLI, AUTHOR *LIFE, THE TRUTH, AND BEING FREE*, RADIO SHOW HOST

"As a mother and grandmother in recovery who has been blessed to support and encourage other moms in their journey to recovery, I was moved, encouraged, uplifted, and, most of all, excited to share this book with my children, friends, and members of my group."

—JUDY MURPHY, RECOVERY SERVICES COORDINATOR, FIRST RESOURCES CORPORATION; COFOUNDER, MOMS OFF METH

"This book is raw and real, yet loving and gentle. You will feel understood, validated, and inspired by Joy's wisdom and practical advice. You will want to read this book cover to cover and then keep it on your nightstand for continuous inspiration."

—JANE NELSON, AUTHOR OF *SERENITY AND POSITIVE DISCIPLINE*

"Barbara has a wonderful way of working with moms in recovery and getting them to honestly and openly share their most intimate feelings about motherhood and recovery. She manages to pose the types of questions and concerns that make any mom think about her responsibility to be the best mother she can be. It's not all about young children. As a mom in recovery, I truly appreciated Barbara reaching out to recovering mothers with adult children: those stories were particularly moving because the mothers have learned the art of letting go and letting God. Barbara's use of affirmations and the activities she poses for journal writing are profound and so useful for any mom."

—KATHY L., AUTHOR OF *THE INTERVENTION BOOK* AND *12 STEP*

"Each chapter reminds me of a conversation between women trying their best to overcome addiction while taking care of their children. These women share their pain, courage, regret, pride, and, above all, the utmost love for their children. Joy is clear and nonjudgmental in her writing style. I heartily recommend this book!"

—PENNY HASTINGS, AUTHOR OF *HOW TO WIN A SPORTS SCHOLARSHIP* AND *SPORTS FOR HER: A REFERENCE GUIDE FOR TEENAGE GIRLS*

"From the start, opening *Moms to Moms* is like having coffee and chatting with your best friend. It will truly be a blessing for all those who are lucky enough to read it."

—MARY KORZAN, AUTHOR OF *WHEN YOU THOUGHT I WASN'T LOOKING: A BOOK OF THANKS FOR MOM*

"Inspiring, reassuring, touching, and thought provoking: this was my experience reading *Moms to Moms*. Barbara lets each of us know that what we feel, the transitions we are going through, and the tears we shed are all okay! This is so needed. Bravo!"

—PAMELA MILLER, COLLABORATIVE JUSTICE COORDINATOR, RIVERSIDE SUPERIOR COURT

"*Moms to Moms* is about destined greatness, success, and significance. Filled with extraordinary stories, testimonies, prose, and practical wisdom, this must-read book is a compass to mothers and children all over the world. This treasure is for you when you yearn for encouragement and need a sisterhood of loving mothers."

—DR. ALVIN AUGUSTUS JONES, THE BUSINESS OF WISDOM©; RADIO PERSONALITY

"By sharing real life experiences from women in recovery, Barbara Joy normalizes the situation and gives hope and strength to women and moms struggling with addiction, helping them to focus on positive changes for themselves and their children. This book serves as another great teaching tool for moms in recovery, those contemplating recovery, as well as professionals and individuals working in the field."

—DR. SHARON YOUNEY, PsyD, RAS, BEHAVIORAL HEALTH AODS SPECIALIST; DRUG-FREE BABIES PERINATAL PLACEMENT SPECIALIST; DEPENDENCY DRUG COURT COORDINATOR

MOMS
to MOMS

SHARED WISDOM
from MOMS IN RECOVERY

MOMS
to MOMS

SHARED WISDOM
from MOMS IN RECOVERY

BARBARA JOY

Conari Press

Conari Press
An imprint of Turner Publishing Company
Nashville, Tennessee
www.turnerpublishing.com

ISBN: 978-1-57324-483-1

Library of Congress Cataloging-in-Publication Data is available upon
request.

Cover by Claudine Mansour Design
Interior by ContentWorks, Inc.
Typeset in Goudy Old Style
10 9 8 7 6 5 4 3 2

I honor every mom who has found her way to recovery.
May your life be all that you dream, because you do deserve it!

I celebrate every child who has a mom in recovery.
May your life be happy and healthy.

I pray for every mom who is still out there.
May you find your way to healing.

CONTENTS

Acknowledgments xi

Introduction xiii

ONE   What Are the Best Parts of Being a Mom? 1

TWO   Why Is It So Hard to Be a Mom? 15

THREE   What Values Do You Want to Teach
Your Children? 43

FOUR   What Lessons Have Your Children
Taught You? 65

FIVE   How Can I Take Better Care of Me? 87

SIX   What Legacy Do You Want to Leave
Your Children? 107

SEVEN   Who Has Been a Positive Influence on
You During Your Lifetime? 123

EIGHT   Do You Have a Final Word of
Inspiration to Share? 143

ACKNOWLEDGMENTS

You've heard the saying, "It takes a village to raise a child." It also takes a village to write a book. I am blessed to have a village that offers consistent expertise, support, and love.

Thank you to Jan Johnson, my publisher at Conari Press, who posed the question, "Barbara, do you have another book in you for moms in recovery?" I answered, "Yes, Jan, I do." And that was the beginning of this book. Thank you for trusting me to become the weaver of many strands. Thank you for the opportunity to create another book for moms in recovery. While there are too many to list by name, thank you to every member of your staff on both the West and East coasts. Each of you are exceptional in what you do. I am forever grateful to be the recipient of your expertise, guidance, sense of humor, and open hearts.

Thank you to the many professionals who invited the moms they serve to be interviewed for this book. A special thanks to Judy Murphy for the outreach she provided, which spanned the Midwest to the Bronx.

A special thank you to Steve Maraboli for sharing his poem, "Dare to Be." Your words of inspiration and encouragement were a perfect way to bring this book to a close.

Thank you to my cheerleaders, readers, and computer angels: Ron Crosthwaite, Andrea Alexander, Mary Hirsch, and Laura Brown. Your consistent "go-girl" and "yahoo" attitudes always came at just the right time.

Most important of all, I want to express my heartfelt gratitude to the nearly one hundred moms in recovery who took the time and energy to talk to me and share your stories, tears, and laughter. Each story became a strand of this remarkable weaving, now called *Moms to Moms*. You are loving teachers to me and the many who will read this book. I love and respect each of you. You are strong and determined women. I am honored to have you in my village. This book is all that it is because of you. Thank you for allowing me to be the weaver of your wisdom.

With gratitude,
Barbara

INTRODUCTION

Other than your recovery, being a mom is the hardest thing you'll ever do. It is also the most important and best thing you'll ever do.

Moms share many commonalities. Have you ever heard a mom say any of the following?

"It's so easy being a mom. All I do is pamper myself and veg every day."

"If I get any more sleep, I just don't know what I'll do."

"I have so much extra money left over this month. What shall I do with it? Maybe I'll take a cruise."

Are you rolling on the floor with laughter from reading these statements? This is not what real moms say.

More realistically, moms are saying . . .

"I love my kids, and it is so hard being a mom."

"I never seem to have enough time or money."

"Sometimes I feel really alone."

"I am exhausted. Will it ever get easier?"

In *Moms to Moms*, sixty-six moms in recovery from across the United States candidly and honestly share their experiences, insights, encouragement, and support for other moms in recovery.

Let me tell you about these moms:

They range in age from seventeen to eighty-four.

They span from the West Coast to the East Coast.

They have been in recovery from one to thirty-nine years.

Many races, religious affiliations, and levels of education are represented.

Some have young children with them. Others don't.

Some have grown children, living on their own.

Some gave their children up for adoption. Others lost theirs to the courts.

Some are single moms. Others have partners.

And yet they all have something very much in common. They are all moms in recovery! They are all strong and determined women.

Moms to Moms is a community of hearts captured on each page. It reminds you that you are not alone. You will see yourself within these pages. Moms feel better knowing that other moms have similar past and present experiences.

Each page of *Moms to Moms* reminds you that, while being a mom is hard and takes tremendous patience and determination, you are part of a community with other moms doing the best you can. You are letting go of the past and creating the life you not only want, but also deserve. And you are not alone.

Each chapter of *Moms to Moms* opens with a question. These are the very questions that the moms I interviewed answered. They are questions that I imagine will provoke you to think and reflect. At the end of each chapter, a journaling activity gives you the opportunity to write your thoughts. There are also affirmations. Write them. Speak them. Pray about them. Even if you do not yet believe them to be true for you, treat them as though you do. You may be pleasantly surprised to see what begins showing up in your life when you use affirmations.

Moms to Moms shares responses and offers solutions from moms in recovery. The solutions may very well be the answer you've been praying for in your own life as a mom.

When you want a boost of encouragement, open this book. Within the pages of *Moms to Moms*, you will find someone who is going through a similar experience on this very day, someone to inspire you and remind you that you are never alone.

ONE

What Are the Best Parts of Being a Mom?

FOR ME AND MANY OF the moms within these pages, it is hard to put into words what the best part of being a mom is. There are so many best parts. It is hard to describe the deep and powerful love we feel for our children. When my children were babies, the best part was standing over them as they slept in their cribs at the end of a busy day. Not because they were finally asleep, but because, in those quiet moments, I saw their innocence and felt how deeply I loved them. They were pure, unconditional love, finally snoozing away.

As they grew and became teens, I think the best part was seeing them during their happy times, when they were feeling good about themselves and felt their lives were working.

And then, of course, there were the times when they were in the mood to talk, and I would just sit and listen. Really listen. Often they didn't want my opinion or advice. They just wanted to be heard.

Now, all three are grown and have homes of their own. There are many good parts. Sometimes it's all of us being together around the table and laughing. They all have children. Watching them parent is one of the best parts. There are things I would do differently today, but somehow all three have turned out to be loving, responsible parents. The moments of feeling proud of who they have become may very well be the best part of all.

Better than Ice Cream

Being loved unconditionally by my child is the best. My child sees me as being better than ice cream at times. No matter how bad my day has been, when I walk through the door, my son sees me and gives me that look that only a child can give his mom. His smile fills my whole heart because it is all love for me. His tiny arms hug me with so much strength. That's the best part of being a mom . . . Being seen in the eyes of my child.

—JANET T.

Getting to Know Them as Little People

I am getting to truly know these two little individuals and their personalities. I used to see their struggles as mine. Today, I know the difference. Now it's, how can I help them with their struggle? I love seeing my eleven-month-old develop into who she is . . . she has an attitude now. It's very sweet. The three of us have a lot of fun. They love each other so much. Jackson has never been mean to Piper. He has to take the backseat often because she's the baby.

—KELLY J.

I love watching my little ones develop their own personalities and the love they show for me. We have a shared bond. I love the love they give me, but also love watching them grow, learn, accomplish things, and reach milestones. It's amazing watching them develop their personalities.

—JOANIE S.

That Look in Their Eyes

For me, the best part of being a mom is the incredible amount of love that I get back from my kids. That look in their eyes when I have inspired them or helped them understand something. To be someone they look up to and respect is the most awesome feeling in the world.

—DANIELLE G.

Trust

The best part is when my daughter trusts me. She appreciates when I show up on time and join in her activities. These are not things I did when I was drinking. Now they mean so much to her.

—KARLA M.

Watching Her Grow

Watching the miracle of life happen before my eyes and knowing that I took part in it. Watching my daughter Sadie grow into a beautiful person, learning and experiencing new adventures and feelings, is priceless.

—STACEY C.

The Day I Got My Son Back

The day I got my son back from CPS was the best ever. They took him as an infant from the hospital. I got him back while I was in treatment. I'll never forget the director of the program handing him to me. It was an awesome moment. And then the day I went to court and legally, completely got him back was also a best. It was an accomplishment. I did it! I succeeded at something so important. I'm not going back, because I could lose everything. I've worked hard. I have my

relationship back with my mom, too. She
used to put out missing reports on me and I
would get so mad at her. And now I know it's
because she loved me and was worried about
me. We have a great relationship now. I've
accomplished a lot in just a short amount of
time.

—TINA M.

The Simple Things

Children appreciate simplicity. Actually, most of us do. When
we manage to keep things simple, there is less room for chaos
and overwhelm to step in and take over our days. A wooden
sign that hangs in my office says, Keep it Simple. It reminds
me daily to do just that. It helps me remember not to over-
book myself. It helps me remember that the simple things
are many times more meaningful than the elaborate time-
consuming stuff.

Imagine a gift-wrapped box sitting in front of you. Before
you open the box, you open the card. It's a handwritten note
from the giver of the gift. The words touch your heart. After
you have opened the gift and the card, which one will likely
be more meaningful? Many times, the card with its simple
heartfelt words will have more lasting meaning than what
was in the box.

For me, the best part is just getting to be
there for my kids every day. At the end of a
work day, I can't wait to get home and just be
a *mom*. It's the simple things in life I enjoy

now, like cooking dinner, watching a movie together, playing a board game. Even going to the grocery store.

—KIM K.

The best part is the love I get from them. It's so fun to watch them grow up into the boys they are. They are remarkable kids, and I am so blessed to have kids that are so normal. The best parts are the simple things . . . playing games together, listening to their made-up stories. They love me no matter how much I suck!

—JEN L.

The best part is that, I notice, when I make healthy choices, my daughter really enjoys the simplest of things. I am there to notice it because I am sober. In my addiction, I was never out of bed before she left for school, so we didn't talk or connect before the bus came. Now, every morning I walk her to the bus. She is smiling (most mornings) as she goes off to school, and I feel good.

—MICHELLE B.

The best part of being a mom is getting to feel connected to something or someone who is directly a part of my own soul. A chance to create a new and exciting life, less the pain of circumstances from my own childhood. Some may say that some parents live vicariously through their children, doing things they never got to do as children. I, on the other hand, feel it's my chance to live the life I was always meant to have, less the childhood traumas of being raised in an unprotected, abusive, neglectful environment. It's almost like having another chance to take my own life back through the will of my own children.

—MICHELLE J.

Their Accomplishments

My son recently got two As. To see the accomplishment on his face is the best. He had worked hard, and this was validation of his accomplishment. I love being able to guide my boys and show them the right way to be in this world.

—KATHRYN L.

The Laughing Game

The best part of being a mom is when I see my son laughing that contagious laughter. Those times when he is just himself. That is pure joy. We have a game we call the Laughing Game. We both just start laughing, and it goes on because we are laughing at and with each other.

—MARY G.

Laughter is healing. Have you noticed that you feel better after a good laugh? Often the circumstances that are stressing us are unchanged. But after a good laugh, life just feels a little lighter.

Quality Time

> Everything is the best now that I'm in recovery. I see their needs. I am present for them. Being able to love and show proper affection instead of a hug and kiss and then sending them off to the TV. I used it as a babysitter. Now I play or read with them.
>
> —STEPHANIE K.

Being in My Life

> The best part of being a mom today is the joy my children bring me by still being a part of my life. They never gave up on me. They loved me even knowing that I was the mom who, after their play or any activity, would need to go in her room to nap (I needed a drink or joint), or who, after coming from a family event, would already be torn up and continue once at home. I'm amazed at how, today, it is so easy for them to tell me they love me. Wow, I'm still forgiving myself. They really love me.
>
> —PATRICIA B.

Seeing Their Own Spirituality

Seeing my kids process and use the techniques and lessons that I am teaching them is the best part of being their mom. Probably the most exciting one is their knowingness of their own Higher Power. My sixteen-year-old was having bad visions, demons in his head, and would turn to anger. I kept encouraging him to let those pictures go to his Higher Power. One day he said, "Mom, those demons just turned into angels." I love watching them use breathing techniques and prayer as they go through their day.

—ALDONA D.

A Deep Sharing

Now that they are grown, I am participating in their lives from a distance, vicariously, and they share with me what's going on. They share on a deep level. Now that they are all grown and in their own relationships, we are really close. They had a rough time growing up. Kids are so entertaining. They were when they were little, and they still are.

—CHANDRA S.

Connecting

Many moms shared that feeling connected to their children is the best part. Think of the times when you feel connected to your child and the times when you do not. Often, the circumstances are the same, and yet there can be a feeling of connect or disconnect. The key to the connection is unconditional love—loving them no matter what—and taking the time to really be present with them.

We sometimes don't love our children's behavior, but we always love the children. Make sure that the love shines through.

> Connecting, really connecting with my teens is the best. I meet my children where they are. If one is in his room, I go to him. I listen and try to talk less. Driving in the car with them is a great way to connect . . . there seems to be fewer interruptions and the conversations can go deeper. Dinnertime at the table . . . I have managed to keep the priority of cooking them dinner and eating together as a tradition.
>
> —TINA A.

The God Box

> My child and I have a God Box. We put our worries, fears, and hopes in it, and give them to God. Every Thanksgiving, we open our box and see all of the worries

that have been taken care of, the fears that are lessened or gone, and the dreams that have come true. There are always a few that surprise us, which have been taken care of but not in the way we thought they would be, or which haven't been answered. My son doesn't focus on unanswered ones, and says they will be addressed when the time is right.

I thought as he got older, he wouldn't use this tool as much. Or I thought he might use it to ask for material things. But I see that this is a powerful tool for him. He believes in a power greater than himself, and he likes having this belief.

Another way we connect is at dinner. We sit down every night with nothing else happening. We talk about our day. What was the best part? What was the hardest part? That is our time together, and nothing is more important at that time.

—MARY G.

Reading

We share and read books. We read together, alternating pages. She sometimes shares with me special parts of a book she is enjoying.

—KARLA M.

Music

Sometimes I am playing my guitar and she is playing with her baby doll . . . pure connection and contentment.

—AMIE S.

Recharging My Heart

My boys like to snuggle with me. They grab their blankets and snuggle right next to me. My youngest son gives me hugs and tells me he is recharging my heart. I hold him until we both feel our hearts are recharged. It's so sweet. He came up with this on his own, and it melts my heart when we can recharge each other. With my older son, he's even more snuggly, so he just gets right up next to me and "demands" to snuggle!

—JEN L.

I love Jen's phrase: recharging my heart. Hugs, sharing a moment, listening to them—all of these recharge our hearts and theirs too. Hopefully, you've noticed that none of the moms talked about buying them things being the best part, but instead simply being present for their children and loving them for exactly who they are.

I *find ways to connect with my children every day.*

I *appreciate the simple things that my children and I do together.*

I *am grateful for my children just as they are.*

What's the best part of being a mom for you?

TWO

Why Is It So Hard to Be a Mom?

MOST MOMS AGREE THAT IT'S hard to be a mom. Whether our children are young or old, with us or apart from us, being a mom is not for weaklings! In addition to the many other needs we try to meet each day, we also have to tend to our children's needs.

I've never come across a mom, in recovery or not, who doesn't agree that being a mom is sometimes hard. The saving grace is that being a mom is also a gift given to us to be treasured forever.

I'm Outta Gas

The demands, especially with young children, seem never ending. Sometimes both my boys are coming at me with question after question and endless demands that are so important to them in that moment. On a good day, I can hang in there with them. But many days, I'm exhausted. I am empty. I have nothing left to give myself or them. That is when I get testy and cranky. I want to scream. Sometimes, I want to just go away and hide, but there would be no one to parent them, and so I do the best I can. It's not their fault. They're just kids and they have needs. A car won't run if it's out of gas. A mom won't run if she's on empty.

—Jen L.

Patience

If only we always had a full supply of patience. Ever notice how, when you are feeling patient, the kids seem to get along better and the day goes more smoothly?

Children push us to the edge. Sometimes over the edge, and that is when the screaming and threats take over. Children don't mean to try us until we lose our tempers. They are not thinking about how their behavior and moods impact the rest of the family. When you are exhausted from being up all night with a crying baby, and just want a few minutes of peace and quiet, they choose to pick a fight with their siblings, or just roll around on the floor and make irritating sounds. Have you ever been trying to get everyone in the car to get them to school and you to work on time, but they just keep dawdling? They are not trying to make you mad or late. They are simply not thinking about your need to be on time.

Parents often say that they are sure their young children are out to ruin their days. In most cases, this is not so. They merely have different priorities than you do, and do not yet have the maturity to care if you are late to work.

> I don't like being the bad guy . . . having to always remind him over and over to pick up his toys, turn off the TV, take a bath. All of those seemingly simple tasks that can wear both mom and child into a frenzy. It is almost impossible, some days, to remain consistent and not give in. He needs me to be clear about the expectations and rules. It would be much easier to just yell at him and give up, but that does not serve either of us well. It's my job as his mom. I am his loving teacher, his guide. He is depending on me to show him and teach him how to be in our world. It's how he learns. I am a very important role model in his life. My actions are as important as my words in parenting Parnell.

> Recently, I was in a very bad mood, and Parnell was so discouraged with his homework.

He kept calling himself stupid and dumb. I started to get frustrated with him, and then I realized we needed to be redirected. We walked to the park. I calmed myself down and we started over. We came back home and sat down and did his homework together. If I had to choose a word to describe the hardest part of being a mom, it would be patience. Parenting is so humbling.

—KERI O.

Sometimes we are so desperate that we demand compliance. Do you ever hear yourself saying, "I want it done now!" or, "Do it because I said so"? Sometimes these statements get the kids up and moving to do what we want in the moment. But over a period of time, they lose their effectiveness, and the kids tune us out. These kind of statements also send a message to the child that says, "I am your boss. I don't respect you." And that is not what moms really want to convey.

I get really restless and uptight. I want something to happen, and happen now. It's hard for me to be patient. I lose my temper, especially with Jackson. It's hard for me to be patient when I'm in the mode of wanting what I want now. Usually it doesn't even have anything to do with him.

—KELLY J.

Sometimes just pausing long enough to count to ten or take a few deep breaths can help. Say a quick prayer for patience: "God, grant me the serenity." Even that one simple sentence can help.

Consistency

If we could keep our voices in a neutral tone and be consistent, our parenting would be so much easier—not only for us but on our kids. When we are consistent, they know what to expect. When they know what to expect, they behave better and are overall more cooperative and happy. If your boss tells you one day to do something a certain way, and the next day completely changes it, and then on the third day is back to the original plan, it's confusing and frustrating for you. It is the same for our children.

> Often, when my kids were teens, I had to make unpopular decisions and follow through, because it was in their best interest for me to do the right thing. Being consistent was exhausting. I think it was the hardest part. They were strong willed and determined, and they just kept pushing.
>
> —SHANNON P.

> The hardest part is staying consistent. Having a routine that fits what I need and what they need is a constant challenge.
>
> —KATHRYN L.

Routines

A routine is more than a schedule. It's a rhythm. Imagine you are in the same job and the same house, with the same partner, and life is just kind of going along. One day you arrive at work and find out you are being laid off. It throws you out of your usual rhythm. Your stress and anxiety increase. You are most likely less patient and more frustrated at home. This is because your routine changed.

Now think about this on a smaller scale for your children. They're in the same school and the same house, with the same parents. One day, you decide to move. Maybe it's to a better house or to be near family. And yet it throws the children's rhythm off, and for a while, they act out more. Change can be hard. Even when it's good change.

The more we keep a child's routine consistent, the better it is for the child. Sometimes just keeping the same mealtimes and bedtime can be enough. This does not mean that the routine can never change.

> I am exhausted. Shouldn't a five-year-old and a seven-year-old be able to sleep in their own beds without me, and sleep all night? We have never had a consistent bedtime. They go to bed somewhere between eight and eleven p.m. We are a family of no routine, and play musical beds every night. Help!
>
> —KARON N.

Karon knows what she needs to do. She needs to create a bedtime routine. The eight o'clock hour sounds like it would be an appropriate time for the kids' bedtime. With a little consistent structure, the kids will learn that at seven thirty they begin brushing their teeth and putting on their pajamas, and then there will be time for two stories. After that, lights out. And they stay in their own beds. It will most likely be a power struggle at first, but once the kids understand the new routine, everyone will be happier and more rested.

Decisions Are Hard

You must make many decisions not only about your own life, but also about your children's lives. Those who were fortunate to have positive role models when they were children may find decision making easier. The many who did not have positive role models may find it especially difficult in their roles as moms to know when to say yes and when to sometimes say no.

> I didn't have a positive role model when I was growing up. Many parts of being a mom of five are really hard for me, because I truly don't know how it's supposed to be. I want it to be different than how I was raised. Daily, I feel lost, not knowing what a loving mom would do.
>
> —COLLEEN A.

> The hardest part of being a mom is making decisions. I can't seem to respond when my children want something. I usually say maybe or that I will have to think about it. I have

made so many bad choices in the past. I am
not sure what the right answer is, so I have
to think about it before I say yes or no.

—Kim K.

While this is hard for Kim, she is wise to take the time
to think the situation over before making a decision. It is
important to take some time to mull things over rather
than deciding something in the moment and then later
realizing you made the wrong choice. If you are not sure if
something is going to happen, it is far better to tell them
you will let them know as soon as you know than to disap-
point them.

Many of your children are rebuilding their trust in you. I
was recently working with a mom whose young children usually visited on Tuesday and Friday. One Tuesday, at the end of
their visit, she innocently said, "I'll see you on Friday." When
Friday came, she was sick and had to postpone the visit. The
kids were too young to understand that there was a legitimate
reason. They were confused, disappointed, and mad at their
mom. Sometimes it is better to say, "I will see you next time,"
than to give them a definitive that might or might not actually happen.

The Constant Bickering

Children's constant bickering, arguing, and fighting can wear
almost anyone down, even the kids themselves. They seem
to have a never-ending supply of energy for harassing their
siblings.

My kids fight from the minute they get up in the morning until they finally go to sleep at night. Or at least it feels that way. I can't understand why they hate each other.

—JENNIFER F.

I don't think your kids hate each other at all. There's good news and bad news about sibling rivalry. The good news is that it's normal. The bad news is that it's here to stay. Sibling rivalry is a way for kids to get their parents' attention and approval.

My eight-year-old daughter and my three-year-old son visit sibling rivalry often. I give each of my children some alone time away from each other. I make some "us" time with me, my husband, and one of the children once or twice a week. Summer and vacations are hard, because they spend more time together than when my daughter is in school. They get along better when they don't spend quite so much time together. It seems to work when they are not together 24-7.

—STACI M.

Guilt, Shame, Fear, and Forgiveness

The feelings of guilt and shame are a significant part of what moms in recovery deal with. You may be holding on to regrets about your past.

Letting go of the guilt and shame from the past is so hard for me. I wasn't around for her when she was little and sometimes I don't feel like I deserve to have her back.

—JENNY D.

While we can understand this mom's feelings, they are not benefiting her or her daughter. It can be continuous work to keep letting go of the past. If you want more insight into and support on this subject, read chapter three, entitled, "Good Bye Guilt and Shame. Hello Pride and Peace," in my book, *Easy Does It, Mom*. It will give you some great tools for working through the guilt.

My oldest daughter is twenty-three, and wants nothing to do with me. I was not a mom to her. I deal with this pain daily. The guilt and shame are always with me. I miss her. I want her to be a part of my life. I pray every day that she'll forgive me and want me in her life. I believe it's possible, because my sixteen-year-old daughter has come back into my life after many years of being estranged from me. She lives with me now. We are building a wonderful and close relationship. She has forgiven me, or is at least in the process. I remind myself that my older daughter has her own Higher Power. I am powerless over her. The best that I can do is to stay strong in my recovery, to keep doing what

I'm doing. Hopefully one day both of us will find forgiveness for me.

—Tina M.

I wasn't there for my kids, and now I realize how much I missed out on while in my addiction. I am still coming to terms with the effects that my using still has on my children. Seeing their behavior and difficulties because of my poor choices makes it very hard for me to forgive myself.

—Brenda C.

Sometimes doubt and fear set in that I cannot live up to all that I see in my child's eyes when he looks at me. The self-doubt creeps in every now and then, saying that I can't be a good mother because of my past addiction. I get so afraid because of the responsibility that I have for this little person who thinks the world of me. At times, I am just like a little, scared child, wondering if everything will be all right this time.

—Janet T.

Being a Single Mom

The hardest part for me in being a mom is watching my daughter suffer any pain or discomfort. It's really hard to play both parenting roles. My heart aches when she asks for her daddy. I beat myself up a lot when it comes to trying to pick up the slack of the other parent. I finally came to the realization that I can't change anyone but myself, and that *I am enough.*

—STACEY C.

When My Child Hurts

When Tim, age fourteen, hurts, and I can't take it away, it's hard for me. Sometimes he feels sad and angry that he doesn't have his dad in his life. All I can do is be there for him and try to understand. When he was younger, his father told him he couldn't do things right or be successful. The look on his face showed how he felt. I imagine he was asking himself, "What's wrong with me? Why am I not enough?" The negativity really hurt his self-esteem.

There are times when I wish I had someone to help parent him. Having all of the responsibility on me twenty-four hours a day is a lot. He is growing and changing into a man, but still in that god-awful stage of a teenager. And yet I am the only one who gets all the good stuff too.

—MARY G.

I don't want my kids to ever hurt as I have, and that's almost impossible to prevent. I want them to have a painless childhood. Making mistakes as a parent can be hard on me, as I tend to allow myself to be consumed with them, and that imposes a negative reaction in me, which goes hand in hand with the nagging side of addiction.

The good thing is that I am aware now through this process of healing and recovery. Now I am able to recognize, absorb, and let it pass. I was a foster child at one point during my life, and it was truly a lonely place. I felt alone and abandoned. I had always promised myself that I would be the mom who would break the cycle, and now as I sit here reflecting on this question, I mourn the temporary loss of my two kids to the foster care system. I never took the time to fix the broken little girl or had the strength to walk away from my own poisonous mother. As a result, I have found myself on the other side.

I have found hope for my own future through my kids, the will to live and fight for what I believe in. I know that God could only inspire me by blessing me with my own kids. I know it was the only way to open my eyes. I can be both selfish and selfless at the same

time, but inevitably for a greater purpose: to
be the best mom I can be!

—MICHELLE J.

Finding Balance

I don't know of any mom who isn't looking for ways to find
balance in her busy life. Work, school, home, kids, meetings
. . . the list is endless.

> It is an ongoing struggle to find balance in
> my life for me and my two-year-old daugh-
> ter. How do I do my recovery, work in order
> to make a living, go to school to further
> my education, handle the many day-to-day
> responsibilities of life, and find time for Han-
> nah? It's never enough in my mind. That's
> where the guilt comes in.
>
> I get up early and have a good routine for
> us, and yet there just aren't enough hours in
> the day. Hannah gets the short end of the
> stick. I love being with her, but there isn't
> ever enough time. I want to be able to give
> her a good life; not just materially, but with
> time and attention. I love spending time
> with her and am trying to figure out how to
> give her more. I'm learning to prioritize, to
> let go of things and relationships that drain
> my energy.
>
> —AMIE S.

In this day and age, with all of the digital and advanced technology and busy schedules, I feel we are more disconnected than ever. It's just going to get worse. Being a single parent who works part-time, goes to school full-time, and attends meetings and recovery functions regularly, I am aware that I don't do such a great job at connecting with Sadie as much as I would like. I'm not going to make excuses. I do the best I can.

We have a really good relationship. She can talk to me about anything. There are days when I have to physically tell myself to stop what I'm doing and give her my time and attention. Finding the time doesn't always come easily. We play board games or paint or wrestle around. We are able to connect the most when I shut off my thoughts and give her my full attention. Sometimes I feel like I nag so much that she doesn't hear a word I say. She has learned to tune me out already.

—STACEY C.

Below is a simple exercise that I do a couple of times a year, by myself as well as with the moms I work with. It helps me to see which areas of my life I am satisfied with, and which need attention. There are no right or wrong answers. It's simply a kind of blueprint for us to gauge how balanced we are in our busy lives.

Recently, when I did this exercise, it became clear that while I was satisfied with many parts of my life, I was not having enough fun and recreation. And so I consciously started making sure that something fun was on my calendar each week. I have to schedule fun things just like I do my appointments. Have fun with this.

Your Wheel of Life

Take a sheet of paper and make a circle. Divide it into eight sections. Put the words *Job, Health, Physical Environment, Money, Fun and Recreation, Personal Growth, Significant Other,* and *Friends and Family* into each section. These eight sections represent the key areas in your life.

Imagine the center of the circle being 0, and the outer rim being 10. Rank your level of satisfaction with each area by writing a number between 0 and 10 in its corresponding position between the rims. When you finish doing that in each section, draw a line to join the numbers together. The new perimeter of the circle represents the wheel of your life as it currently is. How bumpy would the ride be if this were a real wheel? This simple diagram can help you to see which areas of your life you are satisfied with, and which areas you might want to change.

When you look at your wheel, you can see which parts may need your attention. If you have two or three areas with low numbers, you may want to start to think about what you can do to bring them into the larger circle. For example, if you have written a 1 close to the inner rim in the Fun and Recreation area (as many moms do), make a list of things you like to do that are fun. And then schedule a time on your calendar to do them! You will be amazed by how having a little fun during your week can make you feel more balanced and patient.

A Sample of What Your Wheel Might Look Like

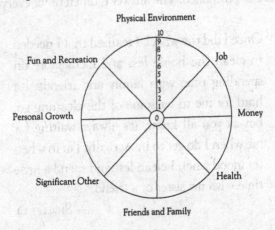

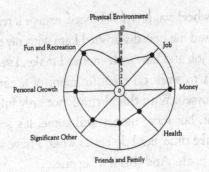

I Need More Hours

I get so tired and never have enough time for me. The kids, work, housework, AA, working out, friends. There are just not enough hours in the day. I struggle with guilt as to how I spend my time.

—JOANIE S.

Many moms feel like Joanie does. Since the number of hours we have each day is not going to change, we need to look carefully at what's filling up our days and see what might be taken off our schedules or postponed. The answer is different for everyone.

> Once I did the wheel, I realized that I needed to clean the house less and focus more on spending time with family and friends. It's hard for me to let some of the cleaning go, but as you all know, it's always waiting for me when I do get to it. Actually, I'm in a better mood when I clean less and spend a little time with my sister or a friend.
>
> —SHELLEY O.

> My wheel was pretty balanced, except it really showed me how dissatisfied I am with my current job and how little money I make. I've set goals to work on creating more of a career for myself. With that, I think not only fulfillment, but more money will come. It's going to take time, but I do better when I have specific goals. And this is a big one.
>
> —GINNY K.

Boundaries

> The hardest part for me is changing the behaviors that I allowed my children to perfect while I was in my disease. It was always easier for me to let them pretty much do

what they wanted. It was easier for me to say yes to everything they asked me because I didn't have time to argue with them. With my thirteen-year-old, I thought, "She's going to do it anyway, so it's better I know about it." With Haily and Emily, it was easier to not make them do their homework than to listen to them whine. I would write a note to their teacher to get them out of doing it.

Now clean and sober, I'm changing these behaviors and stepping up to the plate. My girls are looking at me like, "Where did you come from?" From being sober, I'm learning tools like giving appropriate choices. And setting limits with consequences for the girls. Now, if they don't do their homework, they get a bad grade or have to stay after school and make up the work. That's an appropriate consequence. Hopefully soon, they'll catch on and decide to do their homework.

—SHALANNE A.

I was very codependent and let people walk all over me for most of my life. I now know that my opinion, likes, and dislikes count, and I don't have to do anything I don't want to do or feel uncomfortable doing. I have much healthier boundaries today.

—KARLA M.

I am learning to establish boundaries, to define where my responsibility ends and another person's begins. We don't need to be all things to all people.

—SHANNON P.

The hardest part is living in a transitional home, where my space is shared with nine moms—twenty-one people total. And the time that I want with my family of three, we have to be in the bedroom. Jackson is not a bedroom kind of kid. He needs space. I constantly remind myself that it's not about me. I have to find things for us to do in our small space. It's also hard for me to be organized. I am usually so organized, and when I'm not, I feel like I dropped the ball; life happens, and then I get down on myself. I need to learn how to roll with it. The only way that I am going to really enjoy being a mom is to really roll with the ups and downs of our day. I need to let go of being so rigid and be more flexible.

—KELLY J.

I'll Move Along Ahead

I will find a way

To what I know is right.

I will reach that place

Where I won't have to fight.

The road may have some turns,

Maybe a bump or two . . .

But if I stay aware,

I know I'll make it through!

Keep my eyes well aware

Of things that are there,

And please tell me at times

When I'm wrong.

Help my ears hear your voice

When I need to make a choice,

And please help me

When I need to be strong!

With each passing day,

And as the time goes by,

I'll move along ahead

When I don't know why!

My heart may find a home,

Maybe I'll reach the sky!

I know just what I have,

A willingness to try!

—ALDONA D.

Grown Children

Even when our children are of legal age and out of our homes, it still doesn't mean it's easy to be a mom. The challenges just change. We still worry about them when they are struggling, and we lose sleep when it appears they are making poor choices. They sometimes come to us asking for advice, and when we give it, they get angry and tell us to quit meddling.

For me, being available to listen works best. Many times, I ask my children, "What do you need from me? Do you want me just to listen, or do you want feedback?" If they want me to listen, I turn off my cell phone and anything else that could interrupt us and give them my undivided attention. If they want my input, I give it in the most loving, nonjudgmental way I know how. I try to leave my own judgments and feelings out of the conversation.

Regardless of their ages, they need encouragement and to be reminded they are loved. Sometimes it's enough just to say, "I know this is really hard for you. I also know you are intelligent and caring and you will make the right decision. I sure love you."

It wasn't natural for me to be a mom. Sometimes it's painful for me to watch them make the choices they make. When my daughter was nineteen, she got pregnant. I advised her against keeping the baby. She kept it. That decision turned out to be the best decision she could have made. The baby gave her purpose. Her life turned around because she was a mom. It's still difficult because they are very counterculture, making the choice to be on the edge of things. Their relationship is so enmeshed. It's hard to watch how she parents her child. She's very wise and insightful, but has such a negative attachment. They fight and scream a lot. It's hard for her to step back and be the mom. They're almost like siblings fighting.

It's a miracle that my son is alive today because of some of the choices that he made. Drugs, jail. I've been with him through it all. No stable relationships. They ask for advice but don't want to be judged. It's a fine line. I can advise, but it has to be done in a way that is not judgmental. "Don't tell me what to do."

—CHANDRA S.

I loved being with my kids when they were young. As they became teens, there were challenges and struggles, as there are with many teens. I think the biggest challenge was when they became young adults, and moved out on their own. It was a lonely time for me. They didn't need me like they had all those years of growing up. I came to understand that they still need me, but it's different now. While I am so proud of them for living independently, being caring and responsible adults, sometimes I just miss them.

—CHRISTY V.

I Am Powerless

The hardest part is watching one of my children do some of my old behaviors, like drinking. I am powerless over her. I want to help her understand that there is a better way. But she is not ready for that. I just keep her in my prayers. She always asks me if I pray for her. I tell her yes. Sometimes she tells me that when she's ready to stop, she knows who to ask how.

—PATRICIA B.

Letting go of the guilt I have from the past. I wasn't around for her when she was little.

This is very hard for me. I have so much remorse.

—CHRISTINE G.

Letting go of my children when I wanted to hold on.

—SHANNON P.

Letting go of our own baggage is one thing, but letting go of our children and their choices is sometimes even harder. We need to remember that they each have their own Higher Power and their own journey. The poem below was given to me at a women's retreat nearly thirty years ago. I read it often. There is always at least one sentence in it that helps me in my letting go.

Letting Go

To let go doesn't mean to stop caring, it means I can't do it for someone else.

To let go is not to cut myself off, it's the realization that I can't control another.

To let go is not to enable, but to allow learning from natural consequences.

To let go is to admit powerlessness, which means the outcome is not in my hands.

To let go is not to try to change or blame another, I can only change myself.

To let go is not to care for, but to care about.

To let go is not to fix, but to be supportive.

To let go is not to judge, but to allow another to be a human being.

To let go is not to be in the middle arranging all the outcomes, but to allow others to effect their own outcomes.

To let go is not to be protective, it is to permit another to face reality.

To let go is not to deny, but to accept.

To let go is not to nag, scold, or argue, but to search out my own shortcomings and correct them.

To let go is not to adjust everything to my own desires, but to take each day as it comes and to cherish the moment.

To let go is not to criticize and regulate anyone but to try to become what I dream I can be.

To let go is not to regret the past, but to grow and live for the future.

To let go is to fear less and love more.

—AUTHOR UNKNOWN

❧ Affirmations

I am filled with understanding and patience.

I know when to hang on and when to let go.

I am enough.

❧ Journaling Activity

What are the hardest parts of being a mom for you? What can you do to make each of them a little easier?

THREE

What Values Do You Want to Teach Your Children?

OUR CHILDREN LEARN LIFELONG LESSONS from us. They learn what's important in life and what's not. They learn how to be good people. Most likely, you are much more influential in your children's lives than you realize. They are watching how we behave and walk in the world. While what we say to our children is important, it is also vitally important that we model the behaviors and beliefs that we hope our children will integrate into who they become as they grow.

What values do you want to give your children?

For me, love, family, integrity, responsibility, account-ability, compassion, health, spirituality, relationships, and kindness are some of the important values that I want my children and grandchildren to have.

Family

> My kids and I often go visit my extended fam-
> ily. As soon as we walk in the door, someone
> joyfully takes the baby from my arms and, in
> a welcoming way, points to the table of food
> and tells me to go get something to eat and
> relax. They see the need before I even say
> anything. They know how to welcome oth-
> ers and support me as a single mom. This is
> what family is all about.
>
> —KELLY J.

Kelly's children, from a very early age, are experiencing what it is like to be a part of a welcoming family. In this case, it is their biological family. Often it is instead the like-minded people in our lives whom we meet along the way and turn into family. As Anna says in the paragraph below, she has created her family by being a part of a church community and fellowship.

> My biological family is not in my life. My fam-
> ily consists of the people within my church
> and fellowship that have become family for
> my kids and me. We share holidays. If one

of us needs anything, we are there for each other. That is what family is to me.

—ANNA P.

The day my teenage daughter gave birth to her daughter, all of my children and I were there with her. We were all scared, excited, tired, and hopeful. This experience was new to us and we were blessed to share it all together. While each of us experienced those hours in our own way, we all felt so connected, so close. We loved and cared for each other during the process. It felt good to feel the solidity as a family. We all knew that we were family and were going to love this new little baby!

—TINA A.

Honesty

When our son was a teen, we didn't always like what he told us, but knowing he would be honest when we asked him a specific question helped us to have calmer conversations about emotionally charged issues. We seldom had to second-guess or wonder if he had given us the whole truth. The flip side of this is that we had to respond honestly to his questions, which was sometimes uncomfortable for me.

—SHANNON P.

Our children need to be able to trust us. This trust begins when they are very young. If we are age-appropriately honest with them, hopefully they will grow up as Shannon's son did, to know the importance of being honest.

I remember a lazy Sunday afternoon when my youngest daughter was about five. I was relaxing on the sofa, and when the phone rang, I casually said to my husband, "If it's for me, I'm not home." Sure enough, it was a friend calling for me. As my husband was passing along the message that I was not home, my five-year-old, standing right by the phone, innocently spoke up, saying, "Yes, she is. She's right there on the sofa!" Was my face red! I was embarrassed—and yet, more importantly, I realized I was modeling something that was absolutely contrary to what I wanted to teach my children. Even "little white lies" teach our children that they don't have to be honest. If we can't be honest about the little stuff, how are we going to be honest about the big stuff? That simple experience was one of those moments that I still remember. And of course, over the years, my kids have not let me forget about it!

It would have been better if I had asked my husband to tell my friend I would call her later. These seemingly minor untruths can give our children reason to doubt and distrust us.

I tried to instill honesty in my daughters. I succeeded at teaching this to them, but it later came back to haunt me when they were older and I was drinking. I lied constantly. We think alcohol is such a demon, but for me, nicotine was worse. Kids are taught early in school about the dangers of smoking. My younger daughter pleaded with me for years. She wrote letters saying how she didn't want me to die. She would break my cigarettes into pieces, and I would get so angry. Every time I turned around, she was asking me if I had had a cigarette. I lied over and over. I lost my credibility with her.

—KATHY L.

Not only does being honest teach our children to be honest, but also we simply feel better about ourselves when we live a life of truth. We don't have to cover up one lie with another and another.

No matter what, even when we screw up, be honest. My oldest son always reminds me that we are responsible for telling the truth. My sons are learning by my example. Recently my son brought a piece of gum home from school. I was in rehab at an inpatient facility, and one of the rules was that the kids were not allowed to have gum. Instead of letting him sneak and eat it in his room, I had him turn it in to the office. I was proud of him and me. A piece of gum brought such a valuable life lesson to us.

—KATHRYN L.

Not wanting to take a phone call or a little guy's piece of gum may not seem like a big deal, but these are teaching moments about honesty. When we can be honest about the little stuff, it makes it easier to be honest about everything.

Tolerance

Our world is made up of so many different beliefs, ways of doing things, cultures, and religions. It would be pretty boring if we were all the same. It's important to teach children that, many times, there is more than one way to find an answer, be a family, or live. Some children sleep in beds. Others sleep on mats. Some eat with a fork. Others with chopsticks. No one is better than the other. Just different.

> I want to instill tolerance in my children. We have several close friends who are homosexual men, and they foster children. My kids see that some families have two daddies or two mommies. Sometimes there is one parent and one or maybe many kids. My brother is adopting two biracial children. My boy's best friends are Hmong. It's very important to me, as their mom, to let them have these relationships, because the world is a very diverse, colorful place. I want my sons to know that what's inside a person really shows who they are, not the color of their skin. My husband and I are very opened-minded, tolerant people and this is one of the most important lessons we can give our boys.
>
> —Jen L.

Compassion

Years ago, a mentor of mine said, "Barbara, your work is to teach compassion." I remember thinking, "How in the world does one teach compassion?" Over the years, I have come to realize that I do teach compassion simply by being compassionate. When I am being compassionate, others see it and feel it. It becomes a part of their life experience. My children learned to be compassionate by watching me.

> I want to instill compassion, empathy, and awareness of self in my son. I watch him with two younger boys who live in our neighborhood. Even though they are half his age, he often plays catch or basketball with them. I see him teaching them and encouraging them. When kids his age come around, he doesn't immediately dismiss the younger ones. He spends about ten minutes to wind down with them before going with his friends. No one gets their feelings hurt. Recently, we went on an activity with another mom and two boys his age. One of the boys has autism. I was so proud of how my son watched out for this boy, making sure he didn't wander off and that he got to enjoy the experience, too. I see a kindness in my child that I am very proud of. It's called compassion.
>
> —MARY G.

Spirituality

Spirituality surrounds us daily. It touches the part of us that is not dependent on material objects or bodily comforts. It's in every one of us. Wherever you go, there it is. All we have to do is have open hearts, eyes, and ears. We find it not only in people, but in nature, art—nearly everything we see.

When I go to the ocean or to the trees, I find spirit. It's hard to explain why the tide going in and out, never ceasing, puts me in a place of feeling close to God. Some use different words: God, Higher Power, Universe, Buddha, and so on.

This afternoon, I took a break and walked out into my backyard. The sun was shining and providing just the perfect amount of heat and light. My roses were in full bloom, and a butterfly landed right on top of my head. That was spirit.

If you ever look closely into the eyes of a newborn baby, you may see God. Babies come into our world innocent and pure. They do not arrive with judgment or prejudice. I believe they are born knowing God.

> We must do our part, and God will do the rest. Knowing who I am and where I come from gives me value. When one knows their worth, one can live with purpose. God gives me purpose today. I tell my child to pray about everything. Worry about nothing. We are responsible for our part. Do your best. The outcome is not our responsibility. God is always there to do the rest.
>
> —JANET T.

I want my children to know their Higher Power and that they can always turn to him for everything. My four-year-old daughter has autism. Her speech is very limited. Her very first word was, "Oh God!" On a human level, I think she had gas and her response was "Oh God," but what music to my ears to not only hear her say her first words, but to have it be these two beautiful words. Out of the mouths of babes.

—ALDONA D.

Roberta S. has been in recovery for nearly thirty years. When I asked her about her own spirituality and how it plays a part in her life, she quietly said,

I am a spiritual being. I was born that way, as were you. It's our birthright. My spirituality is as much a part of me as breathing air every day. It shows up in joy, peace, and love. It surrounds us if we just open to it and allow it into our hearts. I try to read something inspiring every day and devote a little time, both in the morning and before bed, to get on my knees and express my gratitude for all of the good things in this world. That's spirituality to me. We have so much and yet take so much for granted.

Mistakes

Mistakes are not bad. They are opportunities to learn. When we look at a mistake as something that we can learn from, there does not need to be shame, blame, or guilt. Everyone makes mistakes.

Most of us were raised to believe that mistakes were bad and that we needed to be punished for them. The punishment only taught us to believe that we were bad and most likely did not teach us how to make better choices next time. Every mistake is an opportunity for growth and discovery.

> I want my kids to really understand what it is to live life, to be happy, understanding, forgiving people with love in their hearts. I want them to know that no matter what they do in life, they are loved, and that it's okay to make mistakes. It's what we do with the mistakes that matters most. I want them to know that, although there is pain and suffering, good things will always come. I want them to know that life is a blessing and that it is truly what we make of it. I want them to appreciate all the small things as well as the grand! I hope my children will someday say to me that they love me and that I was a good mother and teacher to them.
>
> —MICHELLE J.

When talking about mistakes, Jane Nelsen, author of *Positive Discipline for Parenting in Recovery*, describes the 3 Rs of Recovery:

1. Recognize your mistake.
2. Reconcile by apologizing.

3. Resolve the problem by asking yourself or your child, "What can you do next time so that the outcome is different?"

> There is no perfect parent. I want my kids to see me make mistakes (and they have seen plenty of them) and then clean them up. It's how they will learn to handle their own mistakes as they mature.
>
> —KELLY J.

> I believe my kids have learned that people make mistakes and they can change. They have witnessed this is in me, and have watched me working with other moms in recovery as well. They are more apt to be honest about their mistakes, knowing that they too can change. When my son isn't doing well in school, he's able to tell me, and we look for a solution. My teenage daughter came to me and told me she drank one evening and it was scary for her. She knew it was a mistake and she learned from that incident. The next time she became the designated driver.
>
> —TINA A.

> When I was a teenager, we lived in Germany. My mother had beautiful and expensive

Hummel figurines. We used to chase each other around and wrestle. It's one way we connected. One day, I ran into a shelf and the Hummels came crashing to the floor. I froze, standing there with my heart in my mouth, so afraid I was going to be terribly punished. The room got very quiet. My mother stood there and looked at me and said, "It's okay. It was an accident. You are more important than the china." That moment will never leave me.

—CHANDRA S.

Play and Laughter

Now that you are in recovery, many of you have shared that you love playing and laughing with your children. Often, with the many stresses in our lives, we become so serious. It's like a breath of fresh air when we lighten up and enjoy some fun times with our children. Playing with our children is a wonderful way to connect. Playing is not only good for them; it's good for you, too.

Some of the best times for my son and me are when we get to play! To be away from the day-to-day tasks of keeping the house clean, him going to school, and me working. We go to Grateful Dead concerts in San Francisco once a year. We stay with my sponsor in a beautiful hotel and just have fun together! It rejuvenates and reconnects us.

—KERI O.

Children age five and under learn through play. Many times, we can find ways to use our imaginations and playfulness to teach them what we want them to do. When my children were in a whiny mood, sometimes I would start just bobbing my head and moving my lips like I was talking to them but no sound was coming out. It would definitely get their attention, and the whining would disappear and we would end up being silly.

My son had horrendous table manners, and sometimes we would have "Manners Night." We made it very fun, exaggerating things like putting our napkins in our laps, or chewing with our mouths closed. It was a very fun and playful way to go over the good manners rules rather than just being a broken record, saying it over and over.

> Sometimes when I come home from a long day at work, my daughter is crabby. I think, "You haven't done anything today but sit around. I'm the one who should be crabby." But then I remind myself that I am the mom and she is the child, and she has most likely missed me today. Many times, I postpone starting dinner and just sit down and play whatever she wants to for a little while. I am constantly amazed that once she feels connected to me and has had some playful attention, she settles into a project while I fix dinner.
>
> —KAREN K.

As the kids get older, there are games to play, both inside and out. Some kids enjoy throwing the ball outside with mom or dad. I always found the ocean a great place to play as a family.

We could all build sand castles together or bury one another in the sand.

> My kids are ten and thirteen. We have designated Friday night as game night. One child chooses the game and the other chooses what the snack will be for the evening. It is amazing how much fun we all have. There's minimal fighting and lots of laughter. Oh yeah, we keep the TV off and they don't even complain.
>
> — JENNIFER B.

Self-Care

Moms seem to always have something they need to get done—work, school, laundry, cooking, cleaning, paying bills, running errands—you know the list. It's endless. And for most of us, the word self-care doesn't easily find its way to the list.

How often do you wake up and think, "Today I have to get my nails done, take a walk, and finish reading that novel I love, all before I meet my friend for lunch and a matinee?" Can you imagine? No, you can't, because it just doesn't work that way when you are a mom. A more realistic picture is, "I gotta get up at six o'clock, finish the laundry, wake the kids, get them fed and dressed and into the car by seven thirty, drop them off at day care, and be at work by eight. On my lunch hour, I can pay a few bills and make phone calls. At five, I'll run by the grocery store, then deposit my check, pick up the kids by five forty-five, and arrive home by six. Whoops, forgot about soccer practice . . . Gotta drop one off at soccer and then race home . . . feed the dog, start dinner, help with homework, run back and pick the soccer player up. . ." Whew, you get the idea. Somehow you can get lost in the day's bustle. And this is not just one day; this is typical of most days.

Here's the bottom-line reality: if you are not taking care of yourself, you cannot take care of everyone else. Moms are resistant to self-care, saying there's no time. I understand. I also know that when we are not taking care of ourselves, the stress catches up, and soon we are either getting sick or finding ourselves much less patient with the kids. It is the wise mom who finds a way to give herself some quality time and attention on a regular basis.

> I spend a little time each day doing yoga and reading. And then, once a month, I find time to just be with *me!* I never used to want to be by myself, but now I love it. The quiet is good for me. Sometimes I take a bubble bath. Or I go to nature. There's something about being in nature that refuels me. I don't let myself get overwhelmed.
>
> —TINA M.

Many moms do not feel that they deserve time for themselves.

> Unfortunately, I don't feel like I do anything for myself because I was selfish for so many years while I was using. I tend to feel guilty for doing things for myself. I know that this is an area that I need to work on. I am a giver,

not a taker and I keep telling myself I need
to do something for me. Until I start doing
that, I will never truly be happy in life.

—KIM K.

I imagine many of you can relate to Kim's words. As hard as
it is, there is a part of her that knows not only how important
it is, but also that she will be a happier person when she gives
herself a little time and attention.

Have you ever heard the phrase, "If mama ain't happy,
ain't nobody happy"? It's so true. Taking care of you will make
you happier, and when you're happy, your kids are going to be
happier, too.

Friendship / Relationship / Community

What a lonely world it would be if we did not have friends.
Friends support us when we need support. Friends laugh and
cry with us.

Children learn how to be friends by watching us. They
watch the kind of people that we choose to be in relationships
with. Do we choose people with like minds and hearts? And
how do we treat our friends? Are we there for them when they
need us? Do we speak kindly of them when they are in our
presence as well as when they are not?

I call my circle of friends my village. I don't need a
big village, but I need to have that handful of beings that
I know I can call upon anytime, anywhere, and for anything. They are there for me, and I for them. We celebrate
the happy times and support one another through the
dark times.

Who does your village consist of?

What are your relationships built on? For me, it is trust, love, and camaraderie.

Where do you find your friends? Work? School? Church? Fellowship?

> When I finished residential treatment, I decided to stay in San Diego and not return to LA. I had begun to build new friendships with other moms in recovery, and I did not want to give those up. I needed them for support. And besides, we have so much fun together.
>
> —CORRIE W.

> I never really had a real friend until recovery. Today, I have friends that understand and don't judge me for my past. Most people learn how to be friends in grammar school. I didn't ever have friends, because we moved so much and my home life was so full of drama. I am learning how to be a friend. Now I can't imagine going through life without them!
>
> —ALYSSA L.

Responsibility

One thing I consistently witness when I sit with moms in recovery is that they have learned to take responsibility for their past actions as well as their current actions. It takes strength and integrity to say,

While I am not proud of my past, this is what
I did. And I am doing all that I can to clean
up the messes of my past and become a useful and responsible citizen.

—BETH A.

Every time I hear a mom say this, I am filled with such respect
for her. I know that her children are learning from her that
they are responsible for their actions, just as each of us is
responsible for ours.

As moms, we are also responsible for teaching our children to grow up to one day become responsible adults. Chores
are an excellent method for teaching children responsibility. Start when they are young with age-appropriate tasks.
For example, preschoolers can put their toys back onto the
shelf, carry their clean clothes to their room, and help feed
the dog. When they reach elementary school, they can set
the table, unload the dishwasher, take out the garbage, and
so on. By the time they are ten to twelve, they can mow
the lawn, wash the car, load and unload the dishwasher,
and much more. Children who have chores and understand
from a young age that chores are part of being a family will
actually be proud and feel good about themselves when they
do their part.

Don't get me wrong, I am not saying that any children
are overjoyed to have a list of chores before they can go out
and play, but helping out is an important part of being a family and a great way to teach the early lesson of responsibility.

It's never too late to start with chores for each member of
the family, but the sooner you start, the easier it is for the kids
to learn that chores are part of being in a family.

My kids were ten, fourteen, and fifteen when I went into recovery. They had not ever had any consistency or rules. They did what they wanted. Once I returned from rehab, it was very hard for me to make them do anything to help out around the house. It's been a battle, but we are figuring it out. We have a Saturday morning cleaning time. Once that's done, they can make plans with their friends, but not until then. I really can't blame them because I didn't know to teach them when they were younger.

—Cynthia L.

It is also important to teach our children that they are responsible for their actions. We do the best we can to model choosing right instead of wrong and the importance of consistency and follow-through.

We have a homework policy. The kids have fifteen minutes once we get home for a snack and then it's time for homework. They are responsible to be at the kitchen table and if they need help, I'm there to help them. My oldest son kept choosing to not show up. And then at nine o'clock at night would be griping and begging for help. I let him suffer the consequence of not turning in a finished assignment as a way of teaching him to be responsible for getting his homework done. He was so mad several times but now he knows if he wants my help, he has to be at the table during homework time. And most of the time, he shows up. His griping is a pain but I know I need to be consistent because it's preparing him for high school and life.

—CAROLINE P.

Positive Changes Are Possible

I was always told that meth was too hard to get off of. I want their generation to know that they can get off drugs if that is what they are struggling with. There is help out there. I want them to always live in the solutions of life, not the problems. I have showed my children that people can change with the right support and direction.

—AMANDA J.

Sometimes They Fall

Sometimes we have to let our children fall even if it would be easier in the moment to save them. I try to give my daughter the tools she needs to learn how to handle difficult situations. Making new friends, learning new skills, and playing games are all opportunities for children to learn important life skills. As we all know, children can be cruel at times. We live in an apartment complex where there is no shortage of children. I watch and listen out the window at these young children learning to take criticism and peer pressure and turn it into coping and social skills. It is hard to watch, but I can't fight all her battles. There will be plenty of times in her life when her feelings get hurt and hopefully she will respond with dignity and grace when life and people are not so nice.

—STACEY C.

✣ Affirmations

I am a positive and loving role model for my children.

Values are important to me and my family.

I learn important lessons from each mistake.

✣ Journaling Activity

What values do you want to instill in your children? Write a paragraph about each of the values and how you plan on teaching them to your children.

FOUR

What Lessons Have Your Children Taught You?

AMONG THE MANY MOMS I talked to while writing this book, the most frequent response to the question, "What lessons have your children taught you?" was patience! In fact, I think every single mom used the word patience! It does take the patience of Job to be a mom, doesn't it? I suppose that's why our children are such experts at teaching us, giving us daily, sometimes hourly, opportunities to practice this skill.

And why is it that we can usually be patient in other places, like work or with our friends and their kids? But as soon as we are with our own children, our patience seems to disappear.

I was a nurse in a pediatric clinic for many years. I thoroughly enjoyed the parents and kids that came to our clinic each day. One evening, after a long day of seeing sick children, I was putting the garage door up when all three of my children appeared with their demands: "She's being mean. Can't you do something?" "Can we go swimming?" "I'm hungry. What's for dinner?" "You're late." "Who's taking me to soccer?" "Can I have a sleepover tonight?" I wasn't even out of the car yet. I just started yelling at all three of them, and the look on their faces was pure shock. They had waited all day for me to get home, and here I was, not even in the house, and already yelling. It was not one of my better moments.

Hindsight is great, isn't it? If they had just given me ten minutes to get into the house, change my clothes, and then begin with their questions, it would have gone more smoothly. But they were kids and they had missed their mom. Or maybe if I had remembered to take a few deep breaths before putting the garage door up, I would have been able to keep my cool, knowing that they had been waiting for me for a long time.

Patience

You can learn many things from children.
How much patience you have, for instance.

—Franklin Jones

Without patience I would be a raging mess.
It takes a lot of patience and courage to raise
children, with or without another parent.

—Staci M.

When we lose our patience, we become irritable and frustrated. Those feelings can quickly become anger and resentment. Even when you think your children don't know you're mad, they do. They pick up on your energy and emotions more than you may realize. Have you ever been frustrated and happened to look at yourself in the mirror . . . "AAAGGHHHHH! Do I really look that mean?" If we don't find a way to get into a more patient mode, we soon find ourselves yelling and threatening.

By the time my daughter was three, she would look at my face and say, "Mommy, I think you need to take a deep breath." She knew, sometimes before I did, that I was on the edge of losing my patience.

Without trying to, our children push us to the edge. They do not realize how their behaviors can make for a good or bad day.

> When my son was little, he was almost
> ADD and very challenging. He taught me
> to be able to endure more chaos than others might. I learned to go with the flow of
> the day.
>
> —CHANDRA S.

Things will run more smoothly when we accept that we don't have to always be in charge or on schedule. Taking a few extra moments of downtime to tend to the emotional needs of our children can make the day go better. And when things run more smoothly, we are more patient.

Often, we must make a conscious decision to be patient. You know the phrase, "Fake it 'til you make it"? Sometimes that's exactly what we have to do. Act like you are being patient. Behave calmly, using a happy voice.

> One day when everything was falling apart, my daughter said, "Mom, do you want to be right, or do you want to be happy?" I burst out laughing, because that is what I have often said to her. In that moment, I realized not only was she teaching me, but that I needed to pay attention to my own words and lighten up. It was amazing how quickly everyone's mood improved.
>
> —CYNTHIA M.

When you feel yourself losing your patience, or your kid has just pointed it out to you, I encourage you to pause, take a few deep breaths, say a quick prayer for patience, and remind yourself that if you can shift your mood, most likely the rest of the family will too. It is amazing what a few deep breaths can do. Try it. You'll like it!

Have Fun

We moms are often so stressed by our many responsibilities that we forget to have fun. Children are experts at having fun, but also at teaching us that it's not only okay to have fun, it's necessary.

> Hannah teaches me every day that it's okay to enjoy life. She busts out in a song and finger plays, and away we go . . . I

used to sing to her, and now she sings and is teaching me to sing with her. It really does shift my day into a lighter and more joyous day, regardless of how much I have to get done.

—Amie S.

Everything is so amusing to my kids. They are teaching me daily to lighten up. They think the most simple things are so great! I am learning to notice the little things, the simple things that delight them, and find a smile within myself about it, too.

—Carmen G.

Forgiveness

Love and forgiveness are the answer to everything. My children have taught me about forgiveness, how to get past the pain and hurt. Accept people where they are and for who they are.

—Janet T.

I am continually touched at how forgiving children are of their parents. Asking for forgiveness can be difficult for many moms in recovery. The beauty is that once you believe you are worth the forgiveness and ask it of your children, many times they forgive with open arms. Often, our children have forgiven us long before we even ask.

My teenage daughter said, "Mom, forgiveness is the act of letting go. Let go of the idea that it could have been different." I will never forget what I was doing, where I was sitting, in that moment when my seventeen-year-old daughter delivered such a profound message of wisdom and forgiveness.

—TINA A.

Especially if your children have siblings, they are practicing forgiveness daily with one another.

Little ones don't understand what resentments are, and I believe that is because they forgive so much more easily than adults. All four of my children can be playing together just great, and all of a sudden the girls come out, crying their heads off like they were just nearly killed by their brothers. Usually, the boys have taken some prize possession of the girls' or called them a name. The girls' feelings are hurt, and with their huge crocodile tears, they say they hate the boys and will never play with them again. We have a quick family meeting to talk it through, and two seconds later, I hear one of the boys say, "Come in our room and play swords," and every time, the girls say, "Oh yeah, let's go," like nothing ever happened.

—DANIELLE G.

They don't hold a grudge or let it ruin their entire day. What a vital lesson for us to learn from them! Let it go and move on!

Forgiveness is a key component of our relationships. It is our job as the parents to teach our children how to forgive, and to forgive them unconditionally, in order to create the bond of trust. As we model forgiveness of both ourselves and others, our children will also begin living lives of forgiveness, and you will soon see what terrific teachers they are.

My son was in a store with his grandmother, shopping for my birthday. He saw something he thought I'd like, and put it in his pocket and left the store. The next day he said he had not slept well last night. I asked him why. His face got serious and he looked like he was going to cry. I just sat there and waited. "Mom, I wanted to get you something you'd like for your birthday." And he pulled the locket out of his pocket. "Do you like it?" I knew there was more to the story, and asked him a couple of questions. "I took it from Target when I was with Grandma yesterday, and now I don't know what to do. Will you keep it anyway?" He knew the answer before I even spoke. I just looked at him and said, "You know what you need to do. Get your shoes on, and I'll drive to the store." He didn't argue. It was a very quiet drive there. I walked into the store with him and told him he needed to ask for the manager. When the manager came, I stepped back, still close enough for my son to know I was there for him, but far enough for him to make his amends with the man. I don't recall what either of them said. I do recall, after a short conversation, my son handed the locket to the man and shook his hand. I was so proud of my son. Not for stealing, but for doing the right thing. As we drove home, he said, "Mom, that man said that he forgives me for what I did because I was honest with him. I'm glad I told you and that you helped me bring it back. I feel better." In that moment, I knew that my son and I had both just experienced genuine forgiveness.

—SUSAN L.

Live in the Moment

If only we could learn to live in the moment. This is a phrase we often hear, but most of us spend our energy thinking about what may or may not happen tomorrow, next month, and next year, or looking back at what happened yesterday, last month, and last year. I am not saying that we don't have to plan ahead and set goals for the future, but if we could learn to live in the present moment, our lives would be so much calmer.

Many times a mom will say to me, "I am so worried about where I will live next or if I will be able to get into college. What if my kids end up doing drugs? What if? What if? What if?" I am finally in a place where I know that the what ifs don't usually come to be, and that lots of time and energy and needless worry are wasted away talking about them.

One of my favorite questions when sitting across from a stressed and afraid mom is, "Are you okay in this moment?" After a few seconds, the mom will dry her tears and softly say, "Yes." "And what about in this moment?" "Yes . . ." and we go back and forth until she smiles. The smile is a sign that she is back, living in the present.

> Jacob is teaching me to live in the moment.
> Whatever he is doing at any given moment
> is what is most important to him. He is not
> concerned about what he did minutes ago,
> nor what the coming hours will bring. He is
> just in the moment.
>
> —JILLIAN R.

I can hear you saying, "Well, that's fine, because he is just a child." However, there is wisdom in his way of being that we can learn from. Do your very best with whatever you are doing in each moment; the next moment will come—do your best with that moment, too. Somehow we have to learn to not only seize but enjoy the moments, because we will never get them back again. I understand that some moments we would not want to repeat but, in truth, most moments are ones that we will cherish—if we are going slowly enough to enjoy them.

> Parnell often reminds me that the details
> don't matter. I start to get all stressed and
> worked up about something, and he'll say,

"Mom, none of this matters." And he is absolutely right. I feel so foolish that my young
son has to remind me, but I am grateful for
all that he teaches me.

—KERI O.

I was blessed to have a very wise father. When my kids were in
high school, there seemed to be one challenge after another.
Many times, I would call my father in tears, telling him about
the latest challenge with one of my teens. Our conversation
would go something like this:

Dad: Barb, is this situation going to matter a
year from now?

Me: [Sniffling] No.

Dad: Is it going to matter next month?

Me: No, probably not.

Dad: How about next week?

By then my tears were drying and I was chuckling. My
dad had brought me back into the moment. In this moment,
the problem seems like a mountain, but in just a matter of
hours, it will have passed, and all will be okay.

In my early recovery, I was constantly trying to jump ahead and figure out how and
when my kids would be coming back home.
My counselor kept bringing me back to the
moment. She would say, "Only worry about

today. Tomorrow will take care of itself." I used to get so mad at those words, but I knew she was right.

—CINDY R.

Faith / Spirituality

My boys have taught me to just believe. They are very spiritual kids. They believe that God will take care of everything. When people die, they tell me that God just got another precious soul. (Those are their exact words, not mine.) They pour love out of every pore of their little bodies. They believe the world is all about love, and I have to agree with them.

—JEN L.

When my children pray, they do not doubt that it will be answered. They believe. I am learning to be a more faithful person by watching them.

—COLLEEN A.

Listen More, Talk Less

Our children consistently work with us on this lesson. Most of us tend to talk way too much. And what happens when we do? Our children simply check out and we end up frustrated, feeling like a broken record. Do you ever feel like the teacher on the Charlie Brown specials? WAH WAH WAH WAH WAH . . . . Watch your child's face. The expression will tell you if he is engaged in what you are saying or not. If not, stop the talk. Sometimes pausing allows the child to say what he is feeling or thinking.

Jackson has been rude and defiant and mean. I've been talking with his dad about it and then he talks with Jackson about it. Jackson recently spent the weekend with his dad. When I spoke with his dad, he said that Jackson had been exceptionally well-behaved all weekend and they had had a great time together. I sat down with Jackson and the conversation went like this:

Mom: Jackson, why do you think we are having such a hard time getting along? Dad said you were so well-behaved this weekend.

Jackson: Mom, Dad tells me to do something once and you go, "Jackson, Jackson, Jackson," and then you just keep talking, on and on and on.

Mom: OMG.

I realized in that moment that I talk way too much. I already knew that, but somehow I didn't realize how it impacts my children's behavior. That was a huge lesson for me. He told me I nag him all the time. I had no idea he was so capable, to not only convey his thoughts but also to be so truthful. And bottom line is, he was absolutely right on. I do talk way too much. I was doing something so irritating to him, and so he just shut down. It was a humbling moment for me. I know when I'm doing it. I hear myself rambling, and yet I just keep on going. Sometimes when Jackson starts acting out, I feel judged by other parents and so I just keep my mouth going.

—KELLY J.

Kelly put it perfectly. Most of us use too many words. We have about ten to thirty-seven words before our children check out on us. Just for fun, count how many words you use before you finally make your point. The kids appreciate it when we talk less. I do not mean we should give them the silent treatment; it's just that, especially when we want them to do something, we need to try stating it more simply.

For example, you want your kid to hang his bath towel up after showering. Instead of going on and on about the floor getting ruined and how he's making too much laundry, simply say, "Jackson, please hang up your towel." If that's too much, try "Jackson, towel, rack." It sounds silly, but you will be amazed how much more readily they respond when we use fewer words.

It was eleven p.m. My teenage son arrived at the foot of my bed and said, "Mom, I need help with my homework, because I'm having a test tomorrow." My inclination was to start yelling at him about the late hour, his procrastinating, blah blah blah. Instead, I said, "You know the rule. You will have to get up early tomorrow morning if you want my help. Good night." If I had chosen to start with the lecture, it would have turned into a fight and we wouldn't have gotten anywhere. I felt good that I let him know I heard him and that I would help him in the morning if he chose to get up. Sure enough, the next morning at six a.m., he was at the kitchen table, doing his homework. It was a success for him and me. As I dropped him off for school, he said, "Mom, thanks for your help." I nearly fell out of the car. But I was learning how fewer words work for both of us.

—LORIE B.

One of my favorite greeting cards says, "The best thing parents can do for children is to listen to them." (Mr. Rogers.) I notice with my clients that it is often helpful when I sit back and genuinely listen. Really listen, without interruption or judgment of what they are saying. Sometimes just listening and not giving advice is exactly what a person finds most helpful. Often, as the mom, you know in your gut what the answer is, and if given a safe place to talk and be heard, you will come up with the answer that is right for you. Our children are the same way.

My daughter recently came in from a date with her longtime boyfriend. I could tell the moment she came through the door that something was wrong. She didn't say anything, but her body language gave me the heads-up signal. I remember I looked at her and just kind of smiled. She headed for her bedroom. About fifteen minutes later, she reappeared. I turned off the television and motioned for her to sit by me.

Me: Havin' a hard time?

Karen: Mom, I am so confused. Darren wants to date other people. He loves me but says he wants to see what else is out there.

Me: What do you think?

Thirty minutes and a bucket of tears later, she finally felt complete in sharing her thoughts and feelings. During that time, I had not interjected any words, other than a little empathy here and there.

Karen: Mom, I feel so much better. Thanks for being you.

I think what she was really saying was thanks for listening to me and not cursing Darren or telling me what to do. As she got up to head for bed, I did say, "I know you'll make the right decision. You are a wise and beautiful girl!" She hugged me and went off to her room. I was proud of both of us. Her for being able to be honest and share with me, and me for being a good listener.

—BONNIE C.

Praise and Encouragement

We all do better when we have someone to encourage us. The good news is that a little can go a long way.

I spent so much time trying to do the right thing that I didn't realize one of the things I used to tell my children before I started using had stuck with them. In a parenting class, I had learned the phrase, "Tell me what I did right not what I did wrong." Another way to say it was, "Praise the good and ignore the bad." My kids would surprise me by cleaning the whole house and instead of saying great job, I would say, "You forgot to take out the garbage." Or they would mow the lawn, and instead of saying thank you, I would say, "You forgot to do the edge by the fence." One day my son pointed out to me, "Why can't you ever just say good job or thank you instead of being so negative?" I do now and bite my tongue on the rest.

—Kim K.

Have you noticed how you feel when someone thanks you? Usually we feel good and want to repeat that same behavior. A simple thank you can go a long way with adults and children alike.

> I recently lost my job. I was so scared that we were going to end up on the streets. When my daughter came home from school, I told her that my company was closing and that I was out of a job. I began to cry, feeling like such a failure, even though it wasn't my fault that the company was closing. Fear had set in and I felt frozen. My daughter came over and just gave me a big hug and then whispered in my ear, "Mom, you are so strong and smart. You will find another job, and I bet it will be even better than this one. I know you can do this and will be back at work soon, very soon." That is exactly what I needed to hear. Someone believed in me and my ability to find more work.
>
> —Keri D.

I've known this mom and daughter for several years. I've watched Keri encourage and praise her daughter through many trials and tribulations. And now her daughter is giving a loving dose of encouragement back to her mom.

Honesty

My sons have taught me to say what I mean and mean what I say. I had the habit of telling them what they wanted to hear in the moment so that I could avoid a fight. And then, when I went back on my word, of course there was an even bigger battle. They lost trust in me. The boys are in a recovery of their own. Sometimes it's progress, not perfection. When I fall back into my old ways, Jason will say, "Mom, you're gonna break your word again." Even if it's not what they want to hear in the moment, I need to be honest. They are teaching me every day to be honest. And as I am honest with them, our trust builds. I hope that with time, they will know they can be honest with me.

—Kathryn L.

It's Their Journey

There are no guarantees. When our children were very young, I had the illusion that our consistent and responsible parenting would ensure a positive outcome. I considered our children to be a reflection of our parenting skills and a representation of our worth as people.

I have learned that I can do everything right and still have some things turn out wrong. I've learned not to beat myself up so much. I know we did our best and that is the most any of us can do. I do not need to be ashamed when I have done my best. Our children are not miniature versions of us. What is right for us may not be right for them. They have a unique set of talents, abilities, and needs. They will make their own decisions and learn from their choices. They have taught me that they have their own Higher Power, and I am not it.

—SHANNON P.

Accountability

She is teaching me to be more organized and accountable. One time, she was going to an activity and was supposed to bring some household items that she thought no one else would remember to bring. I had the stuff together but left it sitting at home. When I arrived at the activity without the items, she looked at me and said, "Forgetter." I felt horrible. I knew I had forgotten in the past, and she felt like I was repeating an old pattern. Trust is huge. It's seldom recognized when it's there, but when it's not, it can be fearful for her and heartbreaking for me.

—Karla M.

Believe In Yourself

My son has shown me how much love I can hold in my heart. I have never felt anything like that pure love when I looked at my son, just holding and looking, when he was born. It was so strong and powerful. He is now a teenager. He teaches me to see the world with wonder and possibilities. He shows me if you have a dream, go for it. It doesn't matter if people say you can't or that it will never happen. He has a goal to play professional basketball and I still see that dream alive in him even though he has been told by others that he can't. I don't see the word can't in him for anything. He believes in himself, and little by little is showing me to believe in myself.

—Mary G.

My Ways Become Their Ways

All my life I have had arachnophobia, a fear of spiders. When my son was little, he would act like the hero and kill the scary spider for his mommy. As he grew older and was exposed to my reaction to spiders more often, he became afraid of them too. Now ten years old, he won't go near one, and I'm the one who has to be brave. I feel horrible that my son was pushed into the role of savior as a three-year-old and now he's terrified of spiders, all because of watching me and my reaction to something.

On the flip side, I have modeled good things as well, such as being a volunteer and helping others less fortunate. My thirteen-year-old daughter made blankets for babies for a local women's and children's shelter. She bought the material with money she had made on her own. Both of my children have volunteered at the violence shelter on game night with the kids. We painted one of the rooms. They did these things to make other people's lives a little better. I did not realize that they followed what I do and don't do so closely, but they have. I've been clean for nearly six years, and they are still teaching me a lot.

—LAURI A.

Daily Life Lessons

Never underestimate their knowledge. Children know everything—much more than we think they do. My children have told me not to do drugs because they are bad for you, and that smoking is a drug. I have learned how to have fun and enjoy the simple things in life, like a stroll in the park. Taking time to play, ride a bike, look at what is all around me, and be grateful for the things I do have. They show me that the material things are not what's really important. It's about the true joys and the sorrows of what life brings us every day. The sun, our health, sobriety, feelings. I learn something new every day from my children about life itself. I am truly so grateful to have my children today.

—DAWN L.

✣ Affirmations

I respect my children.

I learn valuable lessons from my children.

I enjoy my children daily.

✣ Journaling Activity

What lessons have your children taught you?

FIVE

How Can I Take Better Care of Me?

SELF-CARE IS ONE OF THE most important parts of being a mom. It is also probably the most resisted part of being a mom. We get the mistaken idea that we don't deserve to do anything for ourselves or that we simply don't have the time. Hopefully, after reading this chapter you will either continue to give yourself good self-care or you will be willing to begin.

It is amazing that even a little can go a long way in getting through a day! Imagine that you have a well running from your neck to your belly button. As long as there is some water in the well, you can handle whatever comes your way. However, when the well goes dry, the challenges become overwhelming. Ever notice that, when you are well-rested and have done something for yourself, you are more patient and the day goes more smoothly?

If you won't give yourself permission, then do it for the meaningful people in your life. You will be a more patient, kind, and loving being if there is water in the well. And soon, you'll notice that you really do feel better—as do others around you!

I Know I Should, But . . .

> Unfortunately, I don't do much of anything for myself. I feel guilty for doing things for myself because I was so selfish for many years while I was using.
>
> —Kim K.

While I imagine many of you know exactly what Kim is saying, Kim also knows that it is important to let go of the guilt and start taking care of herself in even simple ways. Kim goes on to say,

> On the rare occasion that I do something for me, I sometimes enjoy a movie with a friend or go for a long walk by myself, and I love to work in my yard all summer long. It gives me peace. I keep telling myself that I need to take better care of me.

There Is Not a Lot of Extra Time in My Day

I don't get much time to myself, so in order to enjoy the chaos of everyday life I try to attend at least one recovery meeting a week, talk about what's going on—big or small—with someone, get out of myself, and help someone else, get enough sleep, exercise—even if just twenty minutes or a walk, eat healthy food, and most importantly, take time to pray throughout the day to keep me sane!

—Stacey C.

Just Say No

When my third child was a baby, I finally learned a very important lesson. It was not only okay to say no, but it was a healthy and wise thing to do sometimes. It was easy to become overextended without even realizing it. I was a wife and mom of three, working and going to nursing school, which was a lot. And yet when someone would ask me to help out with their kids, fix a dinner for someone, or volunteer for one more thing at church, my habit had been to say yes and then either regret it or take my stress out on my family.

At first, the beauty of saying no was not easy. But with practice, I was much better able to keep my own stress levels down, and said yes only when it was truly manageable for me. The good news is that even when I said no, the world did not come to an end!

I learned to say NO, and that it's okay for me to say no. I keep my stress down. For example, when someone asks me for a ride, sometimes I say no. This is totally new since recovery. I've learned limits. It's okay not to give my lunch away to a client.

—TINA M.

Tina gives great examples of small ways to set limits by saying no. It's amazing how others figure out other options and life goes on, even when we say no.

Meetings, Fellowship, and Friendships

Hanging out with friends is also taking care of me. Allowing people to care about me and connect with me has been hard, and yet really great. In high school, it was important to be popular. It mattered how many friends a girl had. I've never had real friends until now. I started drugs at thirteen, and I really didn't know how to be a friend. I was so lost. I didn't believe that anyone would even want to be friends with me. Since beginning my recovery, I am learning how to make a real friend and how to be a friend, too.

—KELLY J.

My main thing is to keep in touch with my AA friends. I am very careful with the

friends I choose, because I know recovery is
fleeting if I don't.

—KARLA M.

I try to get at least one "me" day a week so that
I can sleep in, go to a Moms Off Meth meeting,
go to an NA or AA meeting, hang out with
my sponsor, or just hang out with friends in
recovery. Even though I love my children with
everything I have, it's still good to get away.

—STACI M.

I used to feel guilty getting a babysitter for
the meetings I go to. I felt like I did when
I was using, that I was taking off on them.
Then someone pointed out that while I am
leaving them for a meeting, when I get home,
I will be a much healthier and more patient
mom. That insight has helped me a lot.

—JANE R.

Routines

I try to get up at least twenty minutes before I
have to. It doesn't seem like very long, but it's
very nice. It gives me time to focus on the day,
pray, have my coffee, sometimes even take a
quick shower. When I do this, I am more ready
when the kids arrive at the table, ready to eat! If
I manage to be one step ahead of them instead
of two behind them, we all start our day off

on a better note. It's worth twenty minutes less sleep for me. I can tell they like it, too.

—BARBARA T.

A Morning Routine Starts a Good Day

I fill my cup early in the morning with some yummy coffee. I sit comfortably and write three pages of whatever comes to mind. I practice writing without judgment, without crossing my t's or dotting my i's, without worrying about spelling or rereading or remembering what I wrote. I just write, sometimes broken sentences, incomplete and incoherent thoughts, and sometimes I'm painfully bored by my own writings. I learned this process in *The Artist's Way* by Julia Cameron. Next I do twenty minutes of creative visualization, where I use guided meditation to imagine myself accomplishing my goals.

Then Hannah wakes up, and I give her lots of love and morning greetings. We take our shower. She plays with her bath toys and I say my mantras as I wash my hair. I recite the Light Out of Africa saying by Marianne Williamson, except I say it in first person:

My deepest fear is not that I am inadequate. My deepest fear is that I am powerful beyond measure. It is my Light, not my darkness, that frightens me.

I ask myself, who am I to be brilliant, gorgeous, talented and fabulous? Actually, who am I not to be? I am a child of the universe. My playing small doesn't serve the world. There's nothing enlightened about shrinking so that other people won't feel insecure around me. I was born to manifest the glory within me. It's not just in some of us; it's in everyone. And as I let my own light shine, I unconsciously give other people permission to do the same. As I am liberated from my own fear, my presence automatically liberates others.*

Then we get ready for our day. I get Hannah ready first, and then set her up with some music and fun activity while I get ready. We have a big, healthy breakfast and a very positive attitude in the morning. This sets the tone of our day. I stay in close contact with my sponsor, my fellowship, and my Higher Power. If I'm thinking or feeling negative, I call someone supportive and express my thoughts and feelings. I do the next right thing. It's simple, but not always easy. The rewards are highly rewarding. This is one way to fill my cup. The morning routine is so important as to how the rest of my day goes. I'm learning to stop and ask myself, "What do I need to take care of myself right now?"

—AMIE S.

---

*Adapted from Marianne Williamson's A Return to Love: Reflections on the Principles of "A Course in Miracles", New York: HarperCollins, 1992.

My Lunch Hour

> The only time I know I have for me is my lunch. I get to listen to *my* music. No yelling, no nagging. I get home and I get to watch whatever I want. I can enjoy complete silence if I choose. It's my hour to do as I choose.
>
> —DANIELLE G.

While an hour goes so fast, Danielle has managed to carve it out as her time. I imagine even if there's chaos in the morning, she knows that soon she'll have her hour to rejuvenate. And when she goes back to work, she feels somewhat rejuvenated for the coming hours.

When I was raising my kids, I often yearned to be able to be home alone. I didn't always want to go somewhere. Even to be home alone for a couple of hours, playing my music and cleaning the house, was a way of taking care of me.

A Night at Home

> Last night our family was supposed to go somewhere, and I said, "No, I am not going anywhere. I want to be home with my kids and play a game or watch a movie with them." That was taking care of me. When I don't give to myself, I feel really stressed out. And when I'm stressed, I am not as patient with the kids as I want to be. It's an ongoing process for me. Thursday nights are at-home

night. We don't go anywhere. We eat dinner together and talk. The boys need it too.

—KATHRYN L.

Years ago, a client shared a question her five-year-old had innocently asked one day. They were driving home from an after-school activity and the little girl said, "Mom, do you think maybe someday we could just stay home?" When the mom shared this in a parenting class, she was laughing. The response from the group was not laughter. The little girl was actually saying something important, and trying to help her mom see that sometimes we need to slow down and just have some down time at home.

I do the OA Twelve Steps. I eat well. I stay in close contact with my sponsor and sponsees. I subscribe to healthy magazines, and they remind me how to take care of myself. I get up at five a.m., write down what I ate the day before, five things I am grateful for, five things I forgive myself for, and five things I can give myself credit for. Then I call my sponsor. I get eight hours of sleep. I read spiritual books and novels, too. I do well with a consistent routine schedule. Sunday is my only day at home. I do phone time with family, friends, and sponsees. I often take a long walk with my daughter and cook for the week. I organize and portion all of my veggies and grains, and so I have it done for the week. I'm happy and content with my life.

—CHANDRA S.

Prayer and Meditation

> I carve out even ten minutes a day that are
> sacred. It's my time to commune with God
> for nourishment. Amid all the garbage in
> the world, there is a current of goodness that
> I need to connect with. I'm not always suc-
> cessful, but things work best when I make
> that time.
>
> —SHANNON P.

> I get up at five a.m. every morning and talk
> to God. I am getting to know myself, finding
> out that I am okay and learning to love me
> just as I am.
>
> —ALICIA M.

For me, if I don't take a few minutes before I even get out of
bed in the morning to express my gratitude, it may not happen until the end of the day. I've learned how much better my
day goes when I have consciously either said or written the
many, many gratitudes that I have in my life. It has become
a routine for me, and when, for any reason, I leave it out, I
notice more bumps in my day.

I also express my gratitude for the challenges in my life.
I thank God for the opportunities to learn new lessons and
become a better person, knowing that I am always being held
and shown the way.

Health / Sleep / Exercise

The main thing is that I make sure I see my doctor when I'm supposed to and do what I need to take good care of myself. Living with HIV, I want to be around for those I care about. They give me the incentive to keep my doctor appointments.

—ALICIA M.

The main way I take care of myself is exercise. That's my alone time from the kids, and a necessary time for me, physically and mentally. I also know the importance of getting a good night's sleep. I've tried to push this one many times and regretted it the next day. It has been a hard lesson to learn, because there are so many things to do and just not enough hours in the day. I'm trying to get disciplined about eight hours of sleep and eight glasses of water. Most days I take a quiet time after my youngest goes down for her nap. Even if it's just fifteen minutes, it helps me get through the rest of the day. It gives me some time with God and to recharge my batteries.

Some other things I do for myself are walks, a hot bath, a cup of tea and—even some TV time feels like a break I need. I also call on my partner to help me put the children down for bed a couple nights a week . . . My ideal day of self-care would be a yoga class, a massage, and lunch with friends. Unfortunately, financially these things aren't always possible, and Dad has to step up and watch the kids. When I'm not taking care of myself, especially if I'm not getting enough sleep, I definitely can feel a difference. I start being very negative and seeing everything that's wrong in my life.

—JOANIE S.

We walk everywhere. It's good for the kids, too. Jackson sometimes tells me that he just needs to get some energy out. We put on our shoes, and away we go. Or whenever I feel restless, I say, "Let's go." I tell Jackson that whenever you feel stuck, all you have to do is put one foot in front of the other and go.

—KELLY J.

Reading and Writing

I like to pray, read, write in my journal, light candles, enjoy a cup of coffee, play with my baby, get a pedicure, enjoy the scent of lavender, relax and watch a movie, take in something new or different than the norm, go to a meeting, talk to a friend, get organized, be on time, listen to music, do volunteer work, and hang out with my son and play a game. When I don't do these things, I feel overwhelmed, stressed out, detached from my kids. I'm impatient, irritable, frustrated, lost, and annoyed. When I take time to do these things, I feel the love of my children, relaxed, motivated, inspired, comfortable in my own skin, strong, closer to God, closer to myself, and a better friend, mother, and coworker.

—MICHELLE J.

I journal a lot. I read recovery stuff, but also good nonfiction. Before I turn off my light at the end of the day, I read at least fifteen minutes. It's my way of making sure that I've done at least one thing to take care of me that day.

—JANE W.

I began journaling nearly forty years ago, long before I had ever thought about becoming an author. It is one of my ways of healing the past as well as dreaming about the future. I don't typically write in fancy journals. I usually just grab whatever paper is near and write.

I've used a process for years called "automatic writing." I quiet myself and then ask God a question on paper. Sometimes it may be something like, "What do I need to do about this situation?" or, "What do I need to see or speak that I am not aware of?" I then begin writing without conscious thought or editing at all. Sometimes it's a couple of pages, and then eventually I feel a shift from within, and there, in simplicity and clarity, is my answer. It is a simple and very powerful process.

Music

> Music feeds my soul. I love to sing, even when my kids are holding their ears and begging me to stop! I think they like it!
> —MAKAYLA T.

> We go to church every week. The music is an important part for me. It touches my heart in a way that feeds me. I feel better after church.
> —KERI O.

Even today with the kids gone, I still play music much of the time. My mood and what I am trying to accomplish determine the kind of music I play. If I want to get the house cleaned, I put on something upbeat and dig in. If I need to get inspired, I play something quiet and inspirational. Most of the writing of this book has been accompanied by the same three South African CDs. One is gospel and two are jazz. They have become mantras to me as I write each evening. They feed my soul with inspiration.

Paid Off My Debt and Living within My Means

> This year when I got my tax refund, the first thing I did was pay off all of my debt. I am

debt-free for the first time in eight years. This is huge for me. It was a proud moment when I finished with my final debt collector. This was a very good way to take care of me.

—ALDONA D.

My goal is to be out of debt two years from now. I've taken classes and read books, and the most helpful thing I am learning is not to charge anything at all and to live within my means. I don't carry credit cards anymore. I cut all of them up except for one in case of a real emergency. And my sister is holding onto that one for me. One of my favorite questions that I learned to ask myself is, "Do I need it or want it?" Many times, it's something I simply want and then I check in with myself if it is really within my budget and worth it. I actually feel so proud of myself when I make a good choice.

—SARAH N.

Financial debt can create much stress. It's kind of like gaining and losing weight. It's easy to gain, but not so easy to take off those unwanted pounds. The same is true with debt. It creeps up and then it takes determination and discipline to get rid.

Sarah and Aldona are both on track. They have taken responsibility for their debt and can be proud of their goals.

Skydiving

I think the biggest thing I have done so far
was skydiving. I have done it twice, and wow,
what an experience. I think everyone should
do it at least once a year. In my mind, I had
all these thoughts and things I wanted to
let go of. So right before I jumped out of the
plane I really focused on this stuff. When I
jumped, I let all of it go. It was incredible.
When I got to the ground, I felt like a million bucks.

Really, I think every woman just needs to
be a little bit selfish, once in awhile. And in
doing so, it will help you to take care of you!
—DANIELLE G.

While we can't all go skydiving, I love Danielle's words. As she
said, maybe it could be a once-in-your-lifetime experience. What
a perfect way to let go in a way that you don't on most days.

Me . . . Me . . . Me . . .

I am big on self-care. I love self-care! At least
once a month, I find time to just be with
me! My kids have a sleepover with our best
friends. I never used to want to be by myself,
but now I love it. Sometimes I take a bubble
bath, read, write, or take a nap.
—TINA M.

Self-care is something I learned to do in my sixth year of recovery. I created a "me day." "Me days" are days all about me. I begin my day with a wonderful glass of orange juice and a great breakfast. Sometimes I even go out for breakfast. Then maybe I get my feet and nails done, window shop, take in a movie, or just buy an old movie. The movie has to be a comedy, as laughing is a must. I end my day with a warm lavender bath, candles burning in the bathroom and music playing.

I do this every month. When the money is low (which it is) I change it to doing my own nails and feet, looking at a movie I already have seen, and really laugh, 'cause there is always something I missed the first time around. Sometimes I also turn around days, and have dinner for breakfast. Having pancakes for dinner with bacon is sometimes really fun. I have discovered a million ways to take care of myself. I have not found them all yet, but the fun is in the journey. I encourage my sister-friends to do a "me day."

—PATRICIA B.

A Spur-of-the-Moment Retreat

I awoke yesterday morning feeling like either I had been hit by a truck or that someone had taken my high-energy body and left me with this emotionally and physically exhausted ol' woman. I needed a one-day retreat and I needed it now! I heard the words, "Be of silence and remember who you are." Perfect! Those words became the theme of my retreat. I turned off the phone. Voice mail could handle the messages.

I slept, drank tea, rocked and rocked, just watching the fire. I could not get my mind to quiet. I heard the words over and over . . . "Be of Silence." I needed to write. I took a pad of paper and wrote and wrote until I eventually came to that very familiar shift that occurs for me when I am finally silent. It is when I finally reach silence within my soul and the words are right there for me. I step out of the way and God sends me a message. The chaos and spinning is replaced with clarity, giving me exactly what I need in that moment—the truth, understanding, compassion, the question, the answer—is right there in black and white. I am complete in that moment. My heart and soul are nourished once again. I sit content in the silence.

My retreat was exactly what I needed. My silence and words met up, filled me with love and light, and I did remember who I am. And the marathon of my life continues, but with much gratitude for the gifts I received while on my retreat.

Hopefully as you read these excerpts, you realized that you are already doing things to take care of yourself. And there may be some more that you can add to your list.

Now, take a few minutes and make your very own self-care alphabet. Put a word or phrase by each letter to represent something you can do to take care of you. For example:

A. Attend a meeting   D. Dance

B. Breathe   E. Exercise

C. Candles   F. Friends

A_____	J_____	S_____
B_____	K_____	T_____
C_____	L_____	U_____
D_____	M_____	V_____
E_____	N_____	W_____
F_____	O_____	X_____
G_____	P_____	Y_____
H_____	Q_____	Z_____
I_____	R_____	

❧ Affirmations

I consistently take care of myself.

I surround myself with positive and encouraging people.

I deserve to have a joyful and abundant life.

❧ Journaling Activity

Write about a time when you took really good care of yourself and how you felt.

Make a list of three ways that you will take care of yourself this week.

SIX

What Legacy Do You Want to Leave Your Children?

> What you leave behind is not what is engraved in stone monuments, but what is woven into the lives of others.
>
> —PERICLES

EVERY MOM HAS HOPES AND dreams not only for herself but for her children. We want to accomplish things that make us proud of ourselves as well as have our children be proud of us. We want our children to know and see what we did with our lives. At the end of your life, what do you imagine your children will say about you? What do you hope they will say? Everyone leaves a legacy. Merriam-Webster defines legacy as a gift by will, especially of money or other personal property, or as something received from a predecessor or ancestor from the past. More than money or materialistic things, when I think of legacies, I think of the qualities, the traits, the values that I will leave to my children. Things that will be important to them in creating the lives they want for themselves and their children.

Legacies are important because they influence children's lives. A legacy can either be good or bad, a blessing or a curse. Children learn not only from what their parents say, but also from what they do. You are a vital role model in your child's life. You most likely are more of an influence than you realize. How you walk in the world and who you walk with are going to be part of the legacy you leave your child. The daily structure and decisions you make will all be a part of the legacy you leave your children and grandchildren.

The fact that you chose recovery is an important part of your legacy. I imagine that in itself will say that you were a strong and determined woman.

Modeling Grace and Dignity

I found this taped on the inside of my mother's address book: "Dear God, my children are grown now, and I have wonderful grandchildren and even great-grandchildren. I love them all. God, let me remember that I have lived, loved, and enjoyed this life for many years. Do not let me take away from their enjoyment by complaining about every ache and pain. I have earned them all.

Please keep me from mentioning my swollen joints, stiff knees, dizziness, and poor hearing, and anything else that isn't like it used to be. Help me to remember that I have enjoyed a full and wonderful life and am blessed in so many ways. Now is not the time for me to become a chronic complainer.

Please let my mouth be closed while my ears remain open to hear the fun they are having. Let me remember that I am setting an example for them, and that if I keep quiet, they will forever think that I never had a single ache or pain in my life and that I miraculously escaped the ills of old age.

They will hopefully remember me and say, 'I wish I had her genes. She never had anything wrong with her!' That, dear God, will be the best legacy I can leave my family."

—MAXINE T.

Service

Mom overcame drug addiction. She turned her life around and became someone who was caring and kind. She had a passion to

help others and spent years doing just that
. . . helping others turn their lives around.

—Tina M.

Education

She was a hard worker. She showed us kids
that nothing was out of reach if we were
willing to do what it took to accomplish our
goal. Education is important. She set goals
and achieved them by taking one step at a
time. She never gave up. She was a wise and
kind mom.

—Colleen A.

The majority of the moms that I interviewed for this book
agreed with Colleen. The desire to and goal of furthering
their education was important and consistent. While happiness is not contingent on having a college education, education often opens doors of opportunity in terms of careers and
the ability to make a comfortable living.

Fellowship, Play, and Family

I hope to leave Hannah a legacy of love
and deep, meaningful connections with
other human beings. I gave her the experience of a loving and supportive community and good healthy family support, and
she has and knows the trusting foundation
of her village. I hope to leave her with a

natural inclination to laugh and play every day. I hope she embraces some form of art, whether it be dance, music, theatre, painting, or anything creative. And if not art, that she finds something she feels passionate about, and that she is encouraged to follow her dreams. I hope to leave Hannah with the legacy of family dinners around the dining room table, of a strong sense of life and positive energy in the family home. I hope she knows her worth as a woman, that she loves and respects herself and others. She uses her gifts to serve the world. I hope to leave Hannah with the legacy of a strong faith in God. And a knowingness that she can accomplish anything she puts her mind to. Most importantly, I hope to leave Hannah with an unbreakable, unshakeable foundation on which to stand proud, assured that no matter what comes her way, she is loved and supported.

—AMIE S.

Be a Part of the Solution

Our mom did her best to get her life in order. She used the gifts that she was given by God to go forth and make a difference in this life. We know that we were loved and that Mom did the best she could to help those unable to help themselves. There are so many vulnerable people in this world, and she showed us how to continue to be part of the solution.

—Jen L.

A Loving Heart

We can't all leave a prestigious background or lots of money to our children, but we can leave them a legacy of love.

—Naomi Rhode

I remember my mom for her sweetness. Her pure, loving heart always held me, no matter what. One day, when I was six, someone asked me what love looks like. Without missing a beat, I replied, "Giving my mom a rose." She taught me that love goes past death. Love is all that really matters.

—Keri O.

Do Your Best

She struggled in my lifetime, and did all she could to remain clean and sober. She gave her best to her boys and to the life she tried to live. Mom died clean and sober. She died with willingness, integrity, and an open mind. Her life changed because of those qualities. She gave us a better life, and her grandchildren will never see her as an addict but rather as who she became once in recovery. It won't be, "Grandma's back in jail." It will be, "I love my grandma and being with her." The years of addiction won't have to be a part of their lives. The good will far outweigh the bad.

—KATHRYN L.

Work Hard, Play Hard

I often get caught up in the busyness of life. I don't want my kids to remember me as the one who was always stressed out or uptight. I want my kids to remember camping every year on the sandbank, building snow forts and snowmen, taking bike rides clear across town and stopping for ice cream before heading home, building the race car every year as a family. Those are the important things. I hope they will say, "Our mom taught us that if you work hard, you can play hard. If there was something we wanted badly enough, we could achieve our goal. She taught us to always be true to ourselves. She showed us that we didn't have to go through life always pleasing everyone else. She'd say, 'Life is a book. Everyone has their own story, with many opportunities to write it.' We knew that she loved us deeply."

—DANIELLE G.

Keep On Smiling

> I want to be known as a person who climbed mountains just to make a difference, and never gave up on life! They will say, "She touched everyone's heart she came in contact with and always had a smile on her face, no matter how bad her day was."
>
> —KIM K.

Sometimes we forget that a genuine smile can make the day better, not only for the giver of that smile but also for the recipient. We simply feel better when we smile. Try it today. It can turn your day around in a moment. It can also turn around the day for your children.

I Did the Best I Could

> I don't know how much memory Dayton will have of visiting me in jail, but I hope that he will remember that I turned it (my life) around and kept it that way. I want them to know that I loved them a lot. That I really tried to be a good mom.
>
> —CARMEN G.

It's hard to be a mom. When we let go of the past and do our best in this day, we are on the right path.

The Magic of Life

As a young girl, she learned about the magic of life from her grandfather. It was part of the legacy that he passed down to her and then to me. I know and understand that this magic appears and surrounds us daily. We can call upon it whenever we choose. My mom taught me well.

—KERI O.

Unconditional Love

I suppose my legacy would be unconditional love. My love for her has no limits. I began my recovery for her until I could love myself enough to do it for me. I think she will say she wouldn't want any other mother—just me.

—KARLA M.

The Funny Little Things

She did the best she could with us. She was not as bad as she thought. She was a no-shorts mom. She taught us about forgiveness. We are proud of the woman she became in her recovery.

I hope all three of them will say some funny things about me, like how you should not move things around in my house or put the tissue to roll under. They will have stories of how we lived in the same house but I would mail cards to them. They still find it a little strange, but I think it's nice to get mail.

—Patricia B.

Determination

My mom overcame the struggles in her life without giving up. Even when things got really hard, she kept on. She put what she learned into action. She taught us well. She loved unconditionally. She used her heart to change the world.

—Aldona D.

Living with HIV

I would hope my children would say that I showed them what life is about, living with HIV. I came out and fought for what I believed in on issues that affect us all: family, school, environment. I wanted the very best for them. I showed them what happens when a person lives a drug-free life, and how life has so much to give and how to enjoy it every day. I became a better person. If I was

still using, they would have missed out on
who I was.

—ALICIA M.

Our children see us differently when they are young than
they do when they become adults. Below are the honest
insights about a mom in recovery from her three now-
grown children.

> She always knew the answer to everything!
> When I was a kid and I had any question,
> she always seemed to know the answer. She
> has been an endless source of strength and
> support for me throughout my adult life. She
> pursued her dreams without wavering and
> created what she really wanted in her life.
> I admire this. She always gave me freedom
> to be who I am without judgment (for the
> most part).

> Mom, despite all you have been through in
> life, including the darkness and pain, you
> sit now like a little grandma Buddha in the
> garden, peaceful, tranquil, and darn cute. I
> adore you.

—KAMALA

> She taught me perseverance and deter-
> mination.

—MELANIE

Although my mother had her faults, I have the utmost respect for her. She always did her best. Her achievements in life were great. She was a single mother and worked her way through school. She was always there for me to talk to, to give an objective ear. She has always inspired me to grow spiritually and emotionally, and paved that road with her example and her ability to listen. I am happy with my relationship with my mother. I feel lucky in that my connection with her has always been stable and solid. Her support for following my heart has been indispensable toward my musical career. I may have emotional scars from my early life, when she was depressed, angry, and abused drugs, but her striving to overcome those problems and her efforts to become a better mother added a solid base of trust in her that I cherish.

—ANONYMOUS

Healthy Relationships

She was someone we could trust and rely on in healthy ways. We had an interdependent, not a codependent, relationship. She said no when she needed to. She had boundaries for herself and taught us that valuable lesson. She created wonderful, loving relationships in her life. She modeled this with herself, her husband, friends, and family. She was the best mom ever! She taught us what the roles of a mom and dad are. She modeled good work ethics. She did her best when challenges came up. She was a patient, loving, affectionate, and kind person.

—GINA B.

Inclusive

She had a good time being alive. She loved food, art, and making things beautiful. She loved people. My mom had a gift to be compassionate to those she loved as well as those who were struggling. She tried not only to help them but also to show them a better way. She was always inclusive. She helped people realize that they do belong and have a part in this world.

—CHRISTY V.

Family Matters

Family matters. Our family always had family dinners together. She taught us that everyone has their own challenges, and that it's our duty to help others. She wasn't afraid to be funny and crazy. And funny she was! We laughed a lot. She was well-respected for what she did to make a living. She loved us deeply and gave us the best life she could.

—TINA A.

The Gift of Presence

She came from the depths of hell and overcame all of her demons. She was strong and loved so many so deeply. She helped a lot of people find their way toward a better life. Instead of taking everything she could, she'd give the shirt off her back to someone in need. No one in her life doubted her integrity and commitment to family, friends, and anyone she could offer support to along the way. She was a good daughter and mom and loving mimi (grandmother). Laura gifted those in her life with the everlasting gift of her presence.

—Laura B.

I had the opportunity to talk to Laura's two grown sons and this is what they said:

She was the most honest person I've ever known. She was there for me in many ways. Her advice was honest and not sugar-coated. Our world will not be the same without her.

—Doug B.

Mom was the coolest mom ever. She had been through so much pain, hurt, and struggle, and she still turned her life around and did so much. Love you, Mom.

—Dan B.

Honesty Is the Best Policy

The legacy I would like to leave my children is that honesty is the best policy and love is the best answer. I would imagine them saying, "Even though she was sometimes hard on us, it was out of love. She did the best she could because she wanted us to have a better life than she had."

—STACI M.

A Heart of Gold

Our mom had a good heart. We are so proud to be her children. She always did the right thing when given a choice. She was generous with her time, money, and resources. She fought for victims of domestic violence. She was a courageous woman who faced her fears. She was there for us, as well as her many friends. We all knew we could count on her.

—LAURI A.

✣ Affirmations

I am proud of who I am in this world.

I am a positive role model for my children.

I am surrounded by loving friends and family.

At the end of your life, what do you hope or imagine your children will say about you? Write what you want your legacy to be.

If you have grown children, you might ask them what they think they will say. You may be pleasantly surprised.

SEVEN

Who Has Been a Positive Influence on You During Your Lifetime?

DURING OUR LIFETIME, WE ARE influenced by many people. This chapter is about those special people who come into our lives and leave us with inspiration, hope, and encouragement. Most of us are blessed to have at least a few angels who stand out in our memories for the way in which they've influenced the course of our lives.

Until recovery, maybe you did not have someone that fit into the angel category. Now that you are in recovery and have created a supportive community, I imagine you can think of one or two people at least who have influenced your life in a wonderful way.

Are you a Reason, a Season or a Lifetime?

People come into your life for a reason, a season or a lifetime.

When you figure out which one it is,

you will know what to do for each person.

When someone is in your life for a REASON,

it is usually to meet a need you have expressed.

They have come to assist you through a difficulty;

to provide you with guidance and support;

to aid you physically, emotionally, or spiritually.

They may seem like a godsend, and they are.

They are there for the reason you need them to be.

Then, without any wrongdoing on your part or at an inconvenient time,

this person will say or do something to bring the relationship to an end.

Sometimes they die. Sometimes they walk away.

Sometimes they act up and force you to take a stand.

What we must realize is that our need has been met, our desire fulfilled; their work is done.

The prayer you sent up has been answered and now it is time to move on.

Some people come into your life for a SEASON,
because your turn has come to share, grow or learn.

They bring you an experience of peace or make you laugh.

They may teach you something you have never done.

They usually give an unbelievable amount of joy.

Believe it. It is real. But only for a season.

LIFETIME relationships teach you lifetime lessons;
things you must build upon in order to have a solid emotional foundation.

Your job is to accept the lesson, love the person,
and put what you have learned to use in all other relationships and areas of your life.

It is said that love is blind but friendship is clairvoyant.

—UNKNOWN

We oftentimes don't know who or how we change someone. Many years after my children were grown, I got a holiday card from a woman who owned a small store that I frequented when my daughter was still in a stroller. She wrote how she used to watch me with my daughter and hoped that one day she would not only have a daughter, but would treat her like she saw me treating my little one. I was deeply touched, as I hadn't ever realized that my way of being was impacting her in any way.

It can be helpful to look at our relationships and consider if they are for a reason, a season, or a lifetime. Sometimes when people leave our lives, it helps to understand that they were there for a reason or season. And if we need to leave relationships, it can be healing to try and see what the reason was for the other person's coming into our lives for a period of time.

There are those who come for a reason . . .

Life Is a Journey, Not a Destination

> I have been blessed with two counselors who changed my life. One was tough (I mean really tough). I knew he really cared about me and my recovery. My other counselor, Hayley, told me that she would love me until I could love myself. When I would show old behaviors or thinking patterns, she would look me straight in the eye and tell me she was talking to my disease—then proceed to argue with my disease until the real Karla came back.

Harland, my tough counselor, loved me in spite of myself. You either loved him or hated him. When he was getting deep down into my sickness, he wasn't always pleasant or nice. But I knew this was a man who wanted my recovery almost as much as I did. Sometimes even more. He passed away last year and I miss him.

They changed my life from misery, despair, and hopelessness to the woman I am today. I have learned that life is a journey, not a destination.

—KARLA M.

Kind Words

My auntie Norma was my mom's sister. She was warm, loving, and gentle. When I was a child, she was always kind to me. She'd say, "Christy, you were such a cute baby!" I had never heard those words. I thought I had been an ugly baby. Growing up, I was always accepted in her presence. As an adult, she watched my children and loved them so much. I would come home from work, and they would all be sitting around, calm and happy, just hanging out. She was a teacher and really had the gift. I learned a lot from her.

—CHRISTY V.

They Needed Me

When I was getting high, my brother and little sister came looking for me. I was staying at Saint Marks, trying to get off drugs. They told me they needed me. The looks on their faces told me I had to do something for myself. They needed me to be there for them. They changed my life, and I am there for them today.

—ALICIA M.

If You Keep Doing What You Have Always Done . . .

My counselor, David, used to say, "If you keep doing what you have always done, you will keep getting what you have always gotten." The first time I went to treatment, I never went unless I was high, and made it through without getting caught. And yet his words always stuck with me. So the second time around, I told David that I had been high the whole time, last time, and this was the real me. I asked him to hold me accountable and nail me to the wall if I acted differently.

—KIM K.

Dreams Really Can Come True

I was blessed to have a professional who always listened to me and valued what I had to say. One day, she asked me what I really wanted to do in life, and I told her that I wanted to facilitate my own Moms Off Meth group. About six months later, she called me up and asked, "Are you ready to make your dream come true?" She and three other workers and a cofacilitator worked long and hard for six months on getting everything set up for me to start the first Moms Off Meth group in Minnesota. It's been going for three years now.

—KIM K.

To Thine Own Self Be True

The first person that impacted my life when I became sober was my counselor in treatment. She said, "To thine own self be true." I didn't understand it until after I started really finding out who I was. Now I find myself saying it to my sponsees and other people. To me, it means to always remember to be true to myself.

—STACI M.

The Grammar School Principal

When I was in fifth grade, I had a "boyfriend." We talked on the phone from the time school got out 'til I had to go to bed. I still remember how horrible it was when he broke up with me. And, of course, he chose to do it at school. I didn't want to be the one who got dumped. I went to the office, insisting I was sick and needed to go home. After taking my temperature, the school nurse sent me back to class. Puffy-eyed and sniffling, I slithered back into my desk.

Minutes later I was told to go to the principal's office. I kept trying to think if there was something I was going to get in trouble for. She sat down next to me and asked me what was wrong. I started crying my head off. "Chad just broke up with me for no reason and everyone knows. I am not pretty enough. Maybe I should have kissed him, or maybe I should have done more than that—then he would still be with me." She listened to me and never interrupted me. I could feel how much she cared. She said, "Danielle, he does not deserve you. You deserve much better than him. I know you are young, but what do you want in life?" I told her, "I want to fall in love with a handsome man and I want him to ask me to marry him and I want him to be happy with me forever. That's all." She said, "That's it?" "Yes. That is what I want for my life."

She made me realize that my happiness doesn't depend on others. It's up to me. I can like whatever I want to like and be whoever I want to be. It's my choice. And most of all, I am worth it. I left her office feeling awesome. I didn't need some guy to determine who I was. I was Danielle and that was enough.

—DANIELLE G.

There are those who come for a season . . .

A Good Listener

My sponsor has been a consistent and good influence on me. Even when I relapsed, she never gave up on me. She listened to me. I can share things with her that I can't say to anyone else. Everyone needs to have at least one person that they can share anything with.

—CARMEN G.

Get Mad At the Disease

While I was in treatment, I was always crying to my case manager about my kids, and that it was all my fault. I didn't deserve them, and they would never forgive me. More than once, she'd say, "Blame the disease of addiction, not you. If you want to be mad, get mad at the disease." Over time, those words

helped me shift my anger. I beat myself up
less and less.

—Tina M.

Just Today

A mentor of mine always says, "Just today.
Don't worry about anything but today." She
helped me to surrender over and over. I will
never forget her or her words.

—Tina M.

What wise advice. Have you noticed that usually the things
we worry most about never come to be?

My Gardener

In honor of Chandra

I was a seed that no one wanted

Small and insignificant

In a world that I knew nothing about

No gardener dared to give me a chance

Too tough to grow

Too stubborn to survive

Then she came along

And took me in

She planted me in fertile ground

I was warm

And I felt loved

And began to reach out

Soon the sun shone on me

And every day she came to water me

All the while she spoke to me

Sweet soothing words

Encouraging me to grow

Then one day it rained

And a puddle formed before me

And I saw my reflection for the first time

What a beautiful rose I saw

So colorful that none had ever seen

I think she must have known

How very rare a rose was I

And the garden around me

Was much the same

Many roses are we

The aroma of her garden

Has blessed the community around her

And recognized is she

A very rare gardener is she

Thank you for being a rare gardener for all
of us.

—Aldona D.

Modeled What a Mom Is . . .

I was fifteen, pregnant, and in foster care.
There was a nurse midwife who found

a couple that were willing to take me in. They had nine children of their own and they became foster parents for me. When I turned eighteen, I took my three-year-old and went back to my son's father. Even though they still loved me, they could not support my choice. My foster mom modeled for me what it's like to be a mom, to love unconditionally, to be there no matter what. They also taught me about rules and consequences. I will be forever grateful to them for what they gave me. They impacted my life more than I can ever say. Even though I made some poor choices, they still loved me. They introduced me to God and showed me that I am guided and loved, no matter what.

—KATHRYN L.

She Lit the Fire

She was overnight staff when I was in treatment. She saw the spirit and goodness in everyone that she came across. She believed in our broken spirits. She didn't complain or talk bad about anyone. She really believed in recovery and the recovery process. She lit the fire inside of me. It's never too late. She went back to school in her sixties. I carry what she gave me on with my own clients.

—TINA A.

And there are those who come for a lifetime . . .

The Glue of Our Family

My mom has been a constant in my life. She was always there for me, no matter what. She never gave up on me. She took care of my kids when I couldn't. I remember a time in my life when I thought I never wanted to be like my mother, and that was only because she was trying to keep me from harm by being a caring parent. Today, I am honored when my children and other family members tell me I am so much like her. It tells me that I am doing something right. She is the glue that holds my family together. So when I grow up, I want to be just like her: patient, tolerant, loving, and a woman of integrity.

—LAURA B.

Run Toward the Roar

My mom always said, "Run toward the roar, Tina." What was she talking about? Once I got into recovery, I finally understood. Walk toward your fear. That message was given to me way before I ever got into a twelve-step program. She saw me running away from things that scared me. She has always stood for what she believed in, even if others didn't. My mom stays true to her beliefs and she doesn't budge. The older I get, the more I aspire to be like that. I respect her for believing in something and not waffling. She taught me the importance of family. My mom couldn't do a lot for us materialistically, but she always made us feel special. Like fixing our favorite meal. She still does it today. She'll remember what I liked twenty-four years ago. I liked moon pies, and today, if I went to visit, she'd have a case of moon pies ready for me. She's thoughtful and tender in that way. I had to grow up to really see what she was trying to tell me. I used to get mad because she was so opinionated. Now I know she is a woman of her own beliefs and she is loyal to them.

—TINA A.

Stick with the Winners

I am blessed to have a friend that I know is for a lifetime. Without hesitation, she is my best friend, Tina. She repeatedly talks about sticking with the winners. We first met in treatment. We stuck together through everything and still do. She showed me how to be a friend. When I relapsed, she never judged or looked at me as a failure. She just stayed being my friend. Originally, she didn't want to be sober, but she was clear about the fact that she wanted to get her baby back.

Something happened for her that is unexplainable. She is a positive role model, and so inspirational not just to me, but to many.

—Gina B.

True Friendship

A few days after I interviewed Gina B., I had the pleasure to sit with Tina M., her best friend. She said,

> My best friend, Gina, has greatly influenced me in my recovery and as a mom. We have family holidays together. We are doing really well in our recovery. She's a very significant part of my recovery and my life. I love her and I love having a true friend who is going through similar stuff. Our sons have become friends and are growing up together. I never knew the meaning of true friendship until I got clean. If she ever needed anything, I'd be there for her. She doesn't use me, or want me around because she wants something. She's around me because we're friends that love and care about one another.

I could not help but beam as Tina shared about her friendship with Gina. They used practically the same words as they talked about their friendship. I imagine this may very well be a friendship of a lifetime.

Family Support

My mom was way too involved when I was growing up. We did not have healthy boundaries. I let her be my guide way into adulthood. Our relationship, now that I'm in recovery, is much healthier. She has taught me to be a voice for people who don't have a voice.

My sister has modeled a healthy quality of life for me. She pays attention to what's really important. Not just eating for the sake of eating, but really enjoying it. Her husband is a really great consistent male person in my life. They've been together since I was sixteen. He's a patient, giving person. He's done a lot for me. We have fun together. The two of them have been there when I needed them. They have been there without me having to ask them to support me, and taught me what it really means to support someone. And my kids . . . I don't think I really knew anything about who I was until I had them. They are teaching me, showing me who I am.

—KELLY J.

Sometimes people come into our lives for a season or a reason, and yet leave us with a lifetime lesson. For me, it has not necessarily been about the number of years that make a lifetime friend, but rather what has gone into those years.

A Wise Soul with a Head Full of White Curls

The first time I saw her, she was just weeks old, with a head full of white curls like I'd never seen before. I don't imagine I ever will again. From day one, I had this incredible affinity for this child. I somehow knew that she was to be an instrumental part of my life and teach me important life lessons. I just didn't know what they would be. Our families spent many days together. Wherever she went, she captivated children and adults alike. She was a party always waiting to happen! She was an old and wise soul in a very young child's body. It showed most in her eyes.

One of my favorite memories is the time she climbed on top of a cardboard box, leaned up against my mailbox, and began singing the song from Annie, *The sun'll come out tomorrow. Bet your bottom dollar that tomorrow, there'll be sun . . .*

A few months before her fifth birthday, we discovered that her time on earth was going to be shorter than anyone would ever want. We moved into the cycle of caring for her, in and out of hospitals for many months.

The day came when she spoke, saying she wanted to leave the hospital and go home. Everyone, including this very wise six-and-a-half-year-old, knew exactly what this meant. No more pokes, no more measuring input and output, no more doctors trying to think of one more miracle test that might save her life. Only love. She had definite goals for herself once she got home. She wanted time to ride her bike, go to Kmart and buy her sister the Halloween candy that she had seen (mind you, that was in October and it was now February), and go to her secret beach at the ocean with her family. She did accomplish each of her goals in her final few short days.

The day before she died, her parents heard her saying, "Not yet. I'm not ready." We knew she was connecting with the angels in preparation. This child had been greatly loved by many. She had brought more love and joy to our world in her six years than many do in their lifetimes.

The following morning, quietly, with such grace and dignity, she joined the angels in heaven. We had experienced many times of play and laughter, and now we had entered a time of indescribable, deep, deep pain, in having a child so young, so full of life, leave us.

While her cycle of life was short in years, she lived it to the fullest and taught many of us life-changing lessons.

She taught us that it's not about the number of years that we live, but rather about the quality of the love and joy we have in our days.

She taught us not to sweat the small stuff.

She taught us how to die with dignity and grace.

She did indeed teach us that the sun will come out tomorrow . . . it always does . . .

In loving memory of sweet Carrie.

> Some people come into our lives and quickly go.
>
> Some stay for awhile and leave footprints on our hearts
>
> And we are never ever the same.
>
> —ANONYMOUS

✢ Affirmations

I am blessed with significant people in my life.

I maintain and nurture my lifetime relationships.

✢ Journaling Activity

Write about the person or people who have influenced you in a positive way. What did they do or say? Have you told them how they affected you? Is it time to call or write them?

EIGHT

Do You Have a Final Word
of Inspiration to Share?

SO MUCH ENCOURAGEMENT AND WISDOM have been shared within these pages. This final chapter includes the many words of loving thoughts that the moms I interviewed wanted to share. I simply asked them, "Is there anything that you want to share with another mom in recovery in order to offer her support and encouragement?" Often, with tears in her eyes, the mom would quiet herself and then speak straight from her heart.

When Life Gets Good . . .

Most important, in regards to recovery, don't quit doing it because your life starts coming together. When life gets good, some people stop going to meetings and giving back. Give back what you got. It helps you and others in ways seen and unseen. There are other things we can use besides drugs, men, food, and alcohol. You are doing a great job!

—Tina A.

Nothing Stays the Same

No matter how difficult your life may seem at any particular moment, nothing happens by mistake. Each trial guides and shapes the people that we are. We cannot be who we are today without having experienced the things we experienced in the past. As long as we persevere, nothing lasts forever. No pain lasts forever. Eventually we're going to get through it. It only makes us stronger. No matter who or what may come your way, hold on. There's a light at the end of that tunnel.

—Kathryn L.

Laura's Five Dos and Don'ts

Do be a good listener. Children want to be heard.

Don't make promises you can't keep.

Do the best you can in all things. It's always enough.

Don't settle for anything less than. You can have more.

Do ask for help.

Don't worry about what others think.

Do treat others like you want to be treated.

Don't ever give up.

Do be proud of yourself, no matter how small or big the achievement.

Don't beat yourself up. (You did that enough in your addiction.)

—LAURA B.

Support One Another

I believe that God has a big plan for me. Even if it's only for one person, it will be worthwhile. Last week I shared at a meeting. A woman spoke up and said how much my story touched her. Maybe her child will never have to see her use again because of something she heard that night. Don't think that you don't have anything important to share. You do. Pass it on. One person will help another person, and the healing and recovery for countless moms continues to spread. Open to receive grace. God is using me and he is using you to make our world a better place.

—KATHRYN L.

Reach Out

Being a mom is hard. Being in recovery is hard. See the need. Get out of yourself and see the need, whether it's at a meeting or in a friend. Slow down long enough to see another's face and ask yourself, "What is this mother going through? What can I do for her?" Sometimes I get so overwhelmed. I don't know how to ask, or even what I need. Sometimes I need someone to tell me, "Go take five minutes."

—KELLY J.

Everyone Is Fighting Some Kind of Battle

Despite outward appearances, everyone is fighting some kind of battle. No one is immune to problems, challenges, and lessons.

Life can be difficult. We can expect problems along the way. Hiding those problems from our children does not equip them to manage difficulties when they are adults. As a child, my parents kept everything to themselves. Sometimes, I knew something was wrong. I worried because I didn't understand what it was. As a young adult, I had difficulty rolling with the punches when trouble crossed my path. I believe it is better to be honest and matter-of-fact with our children about what is going on, while assuring them of their safety and well-being.

It is easy to become overwhelmed by our circumstances. My own vision is limited. I believe that the only possible outcomes to the challenges we face are those that I can imagine. I need to leave room for little and big miracles.

Change is inevitable and can be beneficial and instructive. Things are only things, and not our security. I needed to create and cultivate a place within me that was safe and secure, which could not be taken away by changes in my circumstances. I seek nourishment and guidance from my Higher Power by spending time in this very place.

—SHANNON P.

Lessons Learned

Many times I have said,

"I can't go on! Wish I were dead!"

So many nights that I would cry,

So many dreams that passed me by!

But something changed within my mind

When thoughts became a different kind . . .

No longer trapped within a spell;

No longer living life in hell!

Bit by bit, day by day,

I find the path

That lights my way.

Time goes on, life goes by;

I have found

The reason why . . .

Many lessons left to learn

Many roads that I will turn.

And when I don't know what to do

Those lessons learned will pull me through!

—Aldona D.

Do I Want It or Need It?

Delayed gratification teaches self-control. I had to learn it myself before I could teach it to my children. I taught them about money and the difference between "wants" and "needs," and I helped them learn to say no, even when it was tough. Luxuries are readily available, and we are made to feel that we deserve them, need them, and are entitled to them. Learning to live within a budget and involving my children in the planning made it easier to say no to what we couldn't afford. There is a finite amount of money available each month and week. Lay the numbers on the table and explain, "This is what we pay for rent, mortgage, food, heat, savings for emergencies, etc., and this is the amount we have to spend for fun this month." Decide together how that money will be spent (or saved for a future purchase). I can sleep a lot better without excessive debt.

—Shannon P.

Shannon sleeps better because she has learned to live within her means. Our fast-paced, easy-to-charge world makes it easy for someone to suddenly find herself drowning in debt. Consider having one credit card for emergencies.

Other than that, I encourage you to get used to asking yourself, "Do I want it or do I need it?" Often, if we just pause long enough to think about the purchase, we are able to put it back on the shelf and move on. By the time you get home, you will be proud of yourself for not buying something because you wanted it for a minute.

Many moms share that one way they try to get rid of their guilt and shame about their pasts is to buy their kids whatever they want or think they want. This does not work. Countless moms realize that what it does teach the kids is that they can manipulate people to get what they want. It does not help them learn valuable life lessons, and it does not take away the feelings of guilt and shame for mom.

Take Suggestions

> Follow the suggestions of the women that came before you. They will not give you bad advice. Remember how you got to be where you are today.
>
> —Laura B.

Create Your Dreams

> I started out with nothing, living at a battered-women's shelter, scared and alone, not knowing what the future held—but it

had to be better than the past. I got involved in some programs in my community that helped me to learn how to apply for jobs, write resumes, shop thriftily, make new friends, and feel better about my life. I volunteered at the shelter for six months, hoping to land a job there. I put in over fifty applications.

One day, someone from the program I had been in highly recommended me for a job at their agency. I applied and got it! With two felonies on my record, I am working a government job! I have been there five years. They have helped me purchase several cars and a home. I went online and found out how to "do it yourself divorce," started a Moms Off Meth support group, and applied for a grant for our group. I have come far and plan to go further.

The moral here is that you can do anything you put your mind to and more.

—KIM K.

Kim's words remind me that if we keep doing the right thing, and then the next right thing, the universe seems to provide us with gifts and opportunities far greater than we would have ever imagined. Believe me, if anyone would have asked me five years ago if I would be an author of not one but two books, I would have laughed. My plan was that maybe someday when I retired I might write a book. But just as the universe had a plan for Kim, it also presented a different time frame and plan for me. And it will for you, too!

It Keeps Me Clean

The guilt and shame I had from using drugs kept me in my addiction. Now the same thing keeps me clean.

—Laura B.

Remember Where You Came From

Pray every day. I ask God to never let me forget where I came from, to have me always remember my worst day . . . The day they took Jordan from me at the hospital. That memory always gives me the strength to keep going. I need it fresh in my memory. I'll never forget what that forty-five minutes felt like. I've forgiven myself, but still remember how it felt. If I ever forget what that moment was like, I might go back out.

—Tina M.

Dream Mother

A new season is beginning for me, leaving the old behind.

The season passing holds many victories
and falls.

I've overcome great challenges and lost
battles.

I see a new hope and am excited, as if I am
learning to get up on the ski lift.

I will try until it's accomplished or
Simply time to let go and move on.

I will make it to the mountain top

Because skiing down is the best part.

God will do in me a great change.

In currents, I will be washed clean

Of old pollution from the past.

Like a great ocean, I will become a thriving
mother

Full of power and wisdom, peace and
comfort.

I will find meditation and patience in my
own repetitious waves,

Washing upon the shore, again and again.

I will become the mother I've always known, only in my dreams.

—KERI O.

Build Your Village

Most important is to have a community. Therapy, classes, and books may be helpful but are not enough. Build a community of people that you can count on through the peaks and valleys. When my daughter was a teen, she ran away. I was part of a Tough Love community. Someone in the group suggested that I put a note on the door saying that if she wanted to come back, she had to call this other person, who would go pick her up and keep her until we could all meet together. At eleven one night, all of these parents came to my house with my daughter. They supported me and her, too. We all sat and talked and created a contract that she and I could abide by. Some sat with her and supported her. Others sat with me. These people were our community. I hope all moms will create community so that they can support each other in being the best moms they can be.

—CHANDRA S.

It takes a village. If women can break down those barriers of being destructive toward

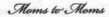

one another and find those mothers and friends in recovery, then we will not have to go it alone. It's so great to love and care for other children and have others love and care for your children. And to do things as families gives our children a beneficial sense of community and family.

—GINA B.

This is one of my all-time favorite quotes, and I want to share it with every mom in recovery. "Want what you have. Do what you can. Be who you are." (From the last sermon by Forest Church at All Souls Church in New York.)

What a wonderful world we will have when we all follow this message.

—GRETCHEN M.

Create a Family

Family is important. If you don't have your biological one, create a family. Share holidays. Make new traditions. Find even small occasions to celebrate.

—MARY G.

In addition to the obvious holidays like birthdays and Christmas and Hanukkah, we sometimes celebrate the first day of each school year by having a back-to-school family dinner. Everyone comes, and we talk about who's going into what grade and what they look forward to.

Recently, we even celebrated when my granddaughter lost her first tooth. We read a book about traditions different cultures have for when a child loses a tooth. Then we wrote the tooth fairy a card. It was very simple and fun.

Many times, it is these spontaneous, simple times together as a family that children remember.

Let Go of the Guilt and Shame

The guilt and shame seem to be a recurring challenge for me. I know the past is the past and I cannot change it. I also know that it is not healthy to keep beating myself up over it. Sometimes I let my son take advantage of me because I feel I "owe" it to him. Every time I let this happen, I am hurting both of us. I am teaching him it's okay to manipulate to get what you want. At the same time, I am letting myself down because I don't have to relive and be punished for wrongs I have made in the past every day for the rest of my life. I can be strong and lead by example. I can have confidence that I am capable and not second-guess myself. I can say no and mean it.

—DANIELLE G.

Pause Before You Leap

It is wise to step back from insanity, rather than diving into it. Being a "fixer," I have a tendency to want to take charge. This creates unnecessary anxiety for me and my family. It also deprives others of the opportunity to grow from their experiences. I have a choice of how I respond to unhealthy situations. I try to review my boundaries before I act.

—SHANNON P.

Feel the Feelings

Life is good. There is so much happiness and joy for you if you will just allow it in. Take a risk. Feel your feelings—they won't kill you. It's okay to feel happy, and it's also okay to cry. A mentor of mine once told me that every time I shed a tear, another part of my heart is healing.

—MARY G.

Live in the Moment

I can get through anything. When I remember to be present in each moment, my life works so much better. Right here. Right now. In this moment, I am okay. Sometimes I say the Serenity Prayer over and over.

—CHRISTY V.

Serenity Prayer

God, grant me the serenity
To accept the things I cannot change
Courage to change the things I can
And wisdom to know the difference.

—REINHOLD NIEBUHR

Willing to Do Whatever It Takes

I was once told, "You've got to be willing to do whatever it takes. Until you face that one thing you are asked to do, and you have to make the choice to say yes or no. You must be honest with yourself. Are you doing this for yourself or for the good of your family?"

—KARLA M.

Allow Yourself to Heal the Past

Often, we mothers in recovery are down on ourselves. There is no room to fit anyone else's opinion of us. Sometimes in my deepest despair and trying to talk my way into recovery, I would tell myself, "This isn't *my* mom's daughter," or, "This is *not* Zoe's mom."

Very seldom did it help. But it did plant a seed. I am an alcoholic. But more importantly, I am a mother, daughter, sister, aunt, granddaughter, cousin, friend, a smile, an encouraging word, a hug, a tear, and a heart so big, sometimes I can't breathe for all the joys that live there.

For many of us, the damage was done before that first drink or drug. To make your recovery the best it can be, give yourself the time to explore the long-ago pain that needs healing. Don't let yourself think that the sexual abuse is over and doesn't affect your intimate relationships. That those degrading words don't affect how you see yourself. That being abandoned didn't scar you. That the hits and kicks healed soon after they happened and there are no lasting injuries. Please don't think your experiences, no matter how long ago, don't matter or are too shameful to reveal, that no one would understand, or that if you don't think about them, they didn't happen. They did. In my experience, those shameful, degrading, painful experiences make me a perfect candidate to understand another's sorrow.

—KARLA M.

Self-Talk

Pay attention to self-talk. Keep the thoughts that are positive and good. Let go of the negative. Replace them with a positive. Use affirmations.

—MARY G.

Get Honest

It's hard for women to be successful in recovery if they have the mistaken belief that they can avoid being honest. Often things happen that may have started your addictions. Maybe you experienced domestic or sexual abuse as a child. Many women don't make that connection. It might have been your way out of horrific situations. Please don't think that it's not a big deal or that you are the only one who had these experiences. Find others who had similar experiences. You will see that you don't have to remain that four-year-old little girl who was molested or continue to have male relationships that are abusive. Be honest in your sharing. Be honest about your past and understand what really happened.

Instead of healing the wounds inside, I wasn't honest about those things. I never wanted anyone to know about my past abuse. I didn't consciously use them as excuses, but I turned to addiction instead. Sick secrets kept me in my disease. Some women don't understand that and still might be resistant, even when they are learning how to be in early recovery.

Are you still holding things back and not getting honest? I know it can be scary to be honest. Find people in recovery who will support you and help you realize that you are not a bad person. You are not alone. Be around people that are safe. Let go of being a victim. It may not be easy to do, but you can do it. Be kind to yourself. Build your self-esteem.

—GINA B.

It's Not Always about Me

When your child is acting out, it is not a reflection on you. Don't take things on that aren't yours. Step back and remind yourself that this situation is not about you. Believe in your children. As long as we continue to model responsibility and teach them how to pick themselves up when they fall, the odds are good that they will one day become such people.

—MARY G.

I remember how proud I used to be when one of my kids got the best role in the school play or made that winning home run. Mistakenly, I thought I should get some of the credit for being such a great mom! Silly me. I also remember when my daughter forged a note and got caught, and my son failed his English class. During these times, I learned that I was parenting them in very similar fashion both when they soared and when they flopped. And it was not that I was a good or bad mom, but simply that they were learning some life lessons. It's humbling to be a mom. I learned to be consistently there for them, whether they were doing well or struggling. My job was just to keep on loving and encouraging them.

Simply Love Them

There's some kind of simplicity in life that I missed for a long time. It seems very simple, learning to love and to be loved. We need to be able to look in our children's eyes and just love them. Not because they are behaving or being good . . . To be able to embrace that part of them is so magnificent and vulnerable. It's a combination of physical, emotional, and spiritual, a whole feeling. Have you ever locked eyes with an infant? That moment of indescribable connection. Sometimes, in the midst of trying to make everything go right, we forget just to take those moments of making a deep heart connection. I used to complain relentlessly to a friend about my daughter. One day my friend said, "Do you love her? I want you to think about how much you love her, and see her as who she is and not just looking at her behaviors." It stopped me dead in my tracks. If I can do that, things will change. We get on such a roll and forget about love, pure unconditional love.

Relationships really matter. Maybe that's why we are here on earth. To love and be loved.

—Christy V.

Mom Now . . . Friend Later

I used to just want my kids to like me. I wanted to be their friend and always get along and always have a great time. It wasn't what either of us needed. I have learned that children need to have rules and be held accountable. It's my job to prepare them for one day being responsible citizens. It's my responsibility to model for them the values that are important, like honesty, responsibility, independence.

Parents are parents and friends are friends. I think when we do a good job being a parent, when they're grown, we can develop a friendship type of bond with them.

—Danielle G.

As my kids reached the double-digit ages, they would often say, "Oh c'mon, you and me, we're friends. Please let me have this or do this." It was a normal and yet subtle way of manipulating me into getting what they wanted. As my kids got older, I would say many times, "Right now, I am the mom. When you're twenty-five and through college, we can be friends."

They didn't always like it, because they weren't getting their way, and yet a part of me always knew that they respected me more because I remained the mom and didn't try to just be their friend. I am not saying that we can't be fun and playful like friends. But we are more than friends. We are the loving moms who are responsible to guide our children safely into adulthood.

Other than your recovery, being a mom is the most important thing you'll do with your life.

Trust Your Gut

At one time, intuition was a vital part of humanity. Humans and animals alike used it for survival. We have spent so much time tramping down our instincts that we no longer seem to preserve our own safety. Recently my daughter was crying, sobbing really, at school, day after day. I asked her what was going on. Her therapist thought it was the upheaval of moving home with me after her removal. I didn't see it that way because I thought things were going well. After some prompting, I found out she was being bullied at school and at Girl Scouts by the same girl. Follow your intuition, especially with your child. Sometimes a mom knows, regardless of what a professional might be saying or thinking.

—KARLA M.

Go for It

When you hear or feel that inner voice, pay attention. It may be telling you, "This doesn't feel right." Or it may say, "Go for it!" If I feel any hesitation, it's not right or was not meant to be. I call it my gut feeling. I had been clean two years, and my husband was still drinking. One day I got this very strong feeling. It was like, if I don't leave now, I will go back to using. I packed up and left my husband without a second thought. I went to a battered-women's shelter. They welcomed me with open arms. I knew then that it was the right thing to do. They taught me how to love myself and take care of myself.

—Kim K.

Pay Attention

Intuition in my addiction was totally whacked. My intuition in my recovery is always on key. When I don't listen to it, I find myself struggling or in the wrong place. Recently, I didn't pay attention to it and I paid the price . . . $336, to be exact. I had four kids in the car with me and my phone rang. I never (hear me, never) talk on my cell phone when I'm driving. My intuition was to pull over and answer it. There was a place on the side of the road where I could have done just that. But instead, I quickly picked it up, talked only a matter of seconds, and hung up. As soon as I hung up, I realized there was a red light coming from the car behind me. Guess who? Once he pulled me over, the officer came up to me and informed me that I had pulled right out in front of him and didn't even see him.

Cop: Did you even see me?

Me: Nope.

Cop: That scares me.

He then proceeded to write out my ticket. A costly lesson, but a lasting one, too. I am grateful for the lesson. God bless my intuition. It tried to tell me to pull over before picking up the phone. Next time, I'll listen and follow. If I don't listen to that inner voice, there I go, getting into some kind of trouble. My intuition teaches me. I am learning how to listen more than ever before.

—ALDONA D.

Plant Seeds

One day, I was at the gas station, and noticed a guy there dealing with a dead battery. I tried to jump it for him and it didn't work.

He said, "That's okay. I'll call my friend. He'll come get me and I'll go buy a battery." I had a bunch of money from my tax return with me. As I was leaving, something told me to go back and give that guy fifty dollars. "Go back and give that guy the money." I knew I was supposed to. I went back.

Me: Can I ask you a personal question?

Guy: Sure.

Me: Do you believe in God?

Guy: Why would you ask me that?

Me: God told me to give you some money for your battery.

Guy: Ugh . . . I guess I believe in God.

So in the store we went and bought the battery.

I don't know if he'll ever believe in God. At least a seed was planted for him to consider that God is always present. They had the battery right there in the gas station. It was a great experience.

—ALDONA D.

Build a Relationship with Your Higher Power

I love my open conversations with God. I have always had the ability to hear, but not always listened or trusted in it. I have often turned away from my intuition, second-guessed or just ignored it, only to be shown by truth unveiling itself through consequences or the invisible finger pointing itself out to me with the "I told you so." Through this process of recovery, my willingness to seek out my relationship with my Higher Power, which I choose to call "God," has enabled me to really be much more in tune with my intuition.

—MICHELLE J.

Children Are a Privilege, Not a Right

I want people to get that children are a privilege, not a right. I used to believe that my children were a chore. They took my time and energy. It has been a powerful movement inside of me since I realized it's not a right. It is a privilege to be the mom of my four now-almost-grown children.

—TINA A.

Tina's words capture one of the most important messages within these pages. Often, with the stresses and busyness of life, we take our children for granted. We forget that they are real people with feelings, thoughts, hopes, and dreams. They deserve the very best we can give them. It is a life-changing moment when we understand that we are deeply blessed beyond words to be called Mom. Our children are a gift given to us like no other. Cherish them. Love them. Respect and honor them in all ways.

Dare to Be

When a new day begins, dare to smile gratefully.

When there is darkness, dare to be the first to shine a light.

When there is injustice, dare to be the first to condemn it.

When something seems difficult, dare to do it anyway.

When life seems to beat you down, dare to fight back.

When there seems to be no hope, dare to find some.

When you're feeling tired, dare to keep going.

When times are tough, dare to be tougher.

When loves hurts you, dare to love again.

When someone is hurting, dare to help them heal.

When another is lost, dare to help them find the way.

When a friend falls, dare to be the first to extend a hand.

When you cross paths with another, dare to make them smile.

When you feel great, dare to help someone else feel great too.

When the day has ended, dare to feel as you've done your best.

Dare to be the best you can—

At all times, Dare to Be!

—STEVE MARABOLI

✣ Affirmations

I am a strong and determined woman.

I am privileged to be a mom.

I have a stable and loving community.

✣ Journaling Activity

Quiet yourself for a moment, and then write what you might say to another mom in recovery who needed a word of encouragement or inspiration. What would you want her to know?

ABOUT THE AUTHOR

 BARBARA JOY IS THE AUTHOR of *Easy Does It, Mom: Parenting in Recovery*, Conari Press, 2009. For the past three decades, Barbara has been providing education, encouragement, and insight to parents, drawing from her clinical background in child development and 15 years as a nurse specializing in children with chronic and life-threatening illnesses. Barbara has a Positive Parent coaching practice in northern California and serves parents in person and by phone and Internet throughout the United States. She is an inspirational speaker and provides trainings for parents, classes, and workshops to many schools and organizations.

Barbara is passionate about assisting parents in raising happy, healthy children, thus creating happier, healthier families. To the moms she works with in recovery she frequently says, "Other than your recovery, being a mom is the most important job you'll ever do." Barbara has 3 grown children and 5 grandchildren.